Arduino Programming for Be

Introduction

Why Arduino?

Basic Terms Worth Knowing

Chapter 1: Arduino – What on Earth Is It?

Where Did Arduino Come from?

Chapter 2: The Key to Understanding Arduino

Understanding What You See

Chapter 3: Know Your Choices

The Crazy World of Arduinos

Time to Shop

Chapter 4: Pick, Buy, and Set Up Your Arduino

Know Which Board Is Right for You

Chapter 5: Coding 101

Understanding the Syntax

Chapter 6: The Arduino Operators

The Arithmetic Operators

The Comparison Operators

Constants

Chapter 7: Understanding the Datatypes

Choose Your Datatype

The Battle of Cases

Chapter 8: Cracking the Code

Some Tips Worth Remembering

Chapter 9: What On Earth Are Logic Statements?

The Logic Statements

Chapter 10: Sensors – How to Work Them

Knowing How to Use Sensors

Diving Deeper

Conclusion

Introduction

When you look at a computer programmer, how often do you think to yourself, "Wow! That guy is a wizard!"? Perhaps on a number of occasions. It is amazing to see what they are capable of achieving, and it is interesting to watch. You can't deny the allure of having the ability to read the unreadable and solve issues that most people can't even begin to comprehend. This is a work that many people may find tedious, but you can't deny its allure. You have to admit that it is awesome.

You may have the appearance of a coder, but you are well aware that this is only the tip of the iceberg. You are one who pioneers new ideas and is creative. You are essentially responsible for developing programs and software, which are utilized by many people in this world. Everything, from video games to autonomous vehicles, from Angry Birds to PUBG, is the result of someone just like you sitting down at a computer and writing the code.

Although many people decide to pursue relevant degrees, in significant part because they are able to do so, some of us have already completed our time at college or university. The vast majority of us just do not have the time to attend classes, much less do so continuously for periods of three to four years. Since this is the case, the majority of us try to stifle our enthusiasm and instead bury it deep inside ourselves. I am sorry to inform you that this is not the case.

If there is one thing that the lockdown has taught us, it is that there is no limit to what we are capable of learning. All we require is a thirst for knowledge and access to effective educational resources. This book will take care of the second portion for you; all you need to do is concentrate on the first section.

Before we get started, I want to share two pieces of news with you: the first is excellent, and the second is even better. Let's begin with the strong point first. You'll be relieved to hear that you just have to become proficient in one programming language.

If you did so, you would be able to begin comprehending most languages, although with some grammatical and syntactical distinctions. You have to understand that the majority of computer languages are founded on a certain structural structure known as syntax. To provide you with some context, I will now define a variable known as "age" in a few different languages:

```
age = 35; // That's Python
auto age = 35; // That's C++
let x = 35; // That's JavaScript
```

You can see how they are quite comparable to one another. It is okay if you cannot comprehend all that is occurring at the same time; nonetheless, I am certain that you can determine that I intend to save the age of 35. Now, you see? It really isn't that difficult.

That was some encouraging stuff. The really good news is that you do not have to immerse yourself in something that is difficult, obscure, or nearly incomprehensible, like an alien language. You could choose to begin your adventure with something that is not as difficult, and that also gives you the opportunity to perform some physical programming. You understood it well when I said "physical programming."

In an ordinary world, whatever a software does, you never get to witness it at work. The power button on your phone is activated by touching the screen. The device begins operating when you turn on a laptop by pressing the power button. A thermometer provides a reading after it has been used. In point of fact, a certain behavior will trigger the activation of the alarm system protecting the home. What exactly is going on here? Here is where the concept of physical programming comes into play, and to get started, there is nothing better than a piece of hardware known as Arduino.

Everyone interested in learning programming as a hobby should begin with Arduino since it is the ideal place to begin. You may utilize Arduino to construct scaled-down versions of projects for your house. It is easy to use, it is incredibly fun, and you really get to play with physical inputs and outputs, which adds an additional layer of interest to the programming.

Why Arduino?

In a word, Arduino is an electrical interface that is built using open-source software. There are simply two components to it. You have your circuit board, which can be programmed in its entirety and functions more like a blank canvas for an artist, and the other component is what computer programmers refer to as an integrated development environment (IDE).

What Exactly Is an IDE?

To put it simply, it is a piece of software that you employ to write code. The program will then transfer the schematics to your circuit board, which is where the code will be stored. After that, the rest is all fun and games. You have access to a wide variety of integrated development environments (IDEs), the vast majority of which are free of charge. The fact that you do not require a supercomputer for this program to function is another positive aspect. Even your aging laptop, which you don't actually use anymore, ought to do admirably in this test.

After you have gathered both of the necessary components, all that is left to do is use a USB cable to link your circuit board to your personal computer. Your computer will begin conversing with your board, and the two of them will quickly become friends. That is the most straightforward explanation I can provide.

You should already be familiar with the meaning of "Hello World" if you have any prior expertise in computer programming. Permit me, however, to quickly explain for the benefit of people who have never written any code before. Newbies are strongly encouraged to write their first program, which is referred to as the "Hello World" program in our community. This exercise aims to write code that, when run, will cause the program to produce the phrase "Hello World." That is each of us' very first attempt at coding a computer program.

That is also something you will be doing with Arduino. It is not nearly as difficult as you would think it is. If we were using Python instead of this language, for example, the code that we are creating would be completely different. After the command has been carried out, "Hello World" will appear on the console (the area where the results are shown). On the other hand, we do not have a screen because we are working with a circuit board. Rather, we are going to put up a display using lights. I am not joking here. Let's put up our very own little light display, right here on our workstation, shall we?

Before we go on, I only want you to read the following, and I don't want you to do it until you've mastered all of the fundamentals and made sure that everything is correctly set up (we will learn all that later in the book). You will need to insert the following bits of code to produce a light show:

```
Const int PinkL = 13;
Void setup ()
{ pinMode (PinkL, OUTPUT); }
Void loop ()
{digitalWrite(PinkL, HIGH);
 delay (500);
digitalWrite(PinkL, LOW);
delay(500); }
```

"Wait a minute, what?"

I was expecting you to be intimidated, and I was right. However, there is no need to be concerned. Almost instantly, each and every line of that code will begin to make perfect sense. However, in an effort to satisfy your interest, I will explain how the code will function.

If you enter this into the coding for your Arduino project and then upload it, it will cause a connected LED to light up for 500 milliseconds, which is equivalent to one full second. After this, the LED will remain off for another half a second in the position that it is now in. The flashing of the LED will continue for as long as you want or until the Arduino runs out of power, whichever comes first.

When you master Arduino, you open up a figurative and physical universe of creative opportunities for yourself. The programming is entertaining, and it enables you to accomplish a great deal more with nothing more than a few basic wires, LEDs, and a few other components. I have seen people use Arduino to construct projects that are quite difficult, such as a home security system that is completely functional, robot pets, and a lot of other things.

To get started, you will need to locate the appropriate type of Arduino gadget for your needs. Once more, we will go over each one of these in greater detail later on in the book; but, just so you are aware, the following are the ones that are now available for purchase:
• Arduino Uno
• Redboard
• Lilypad
• Arduino Leonardo
• Arduino Mega

I will go through their particulars, including their prices and characteristics, to prevent you from feeling lost in the process.

After that, we will also take you step by step through the process of appropriately setting things up and getting started.

Due to the sheer enormous possibilities it offers, Arduino has quickly become popular all around the world. Imagine if a whole industry could fit in the space of a gadget that is a little larger than your hand. If you like, you may take the project to levels that are beyond your wildest dreams. However, between then and now, there is a significant learning curve that you are required to traverse, and that is to study and become proficient in the programming language used by Arduino.

Lastly, I'm happy to share some more excellent news with you. Using the Arduino programming language and your personal computer, you are able to give your computer instructions to carry out complicated procedures, and it will do as you want. In most cases, computers can only comprehend the Binary language, which is more commonly referred to as the language of ones and zeros. It is quite difficult to become proficient in the binary language. It would take me a couple more volumes to teach you the Binary language if we want to study it. There are integrated development environments (IDEs) that can read and convert the code into Binary language for you. The computer would understand the instructions, respond to them, and carry them out exactly as specified. Isn't it wonderful how much easier technology makes our lives?

Because of this, using Arduino is a fantastic method to use to get started, particularly for those who have never done it before. You will better understand the complexity of programming, and your efforts will be rewarded with concrete results. We will be utilizing many examples and exercises, and I will even share some projects with you that you may try to perform at home at certain points during this book.

Oh, I nearly forgot about it. I plan to make programming entertaining, despite the fact that it is sometimes a subject that is really dull. Over this, I will sprinkle the book with a little amount of comedy here and there in the hope that it will pique people's interest in a topic that would otherwise be dull. I have taken considerable effort to ensure that I do not use exceedingly sophisticated terminology without first explaining it. Despite this, you should still be prepared for a few to show up now and again. If you're feeling disoriented, you should turn around and walk the way you came. You might also check out some videos on YouTube to have a better understanding of the situation.

The most important thing to remember is that this situation should be as straightforward as possible. There is a valid explanation for this. You see, if you misunderstand anything or input something that you shouldn't, you risk your Arduino program failing as a result. This is why it is equally vital for me to ensure that you have a solid understanding of the principles.

Basic Terms Worth Knowing

While we aren't exactly starting our book right away, you must get to know some basic terms so that you have an easier read. If required, grab a pen and a notebook to write down these terms and their meanings. These will spring up every now and then, so it is a good idea to understand what they stand for.

•**Loop** – It is just like it sounds. We use loops to create instructions that continue running until they are stopped or when they are no longer meeting the condition that is defined by the user. The code I wrote above, the one for the light show, uses a loop. That is why the light will continue to blink on and off constantly.

- **Microcontrollers** – Microcontrollers are these long chips that have many legs that connect to the board. These are integrated circuits and are essentially computers, only tiny in size. These are used to store data and execute simple programs. They don't require much power to run, which is why you can hook them up with a small battery, and they would work for days to come.
- **Circuit boards** – You need these to make Arduino work. These come in different sizes. It is literally a blank canvas for programmers. You can plug in microcontrollers and many other peripherals using their pins (or legs). As long as the circuit is set up right, it will allow all connected devices to talk to each other and interact. Of course, you will need to solder the connecting pins to keep them in place. We won't be using these as much, though, so don't worry yourself too much here.
- **Potentiometer** – Think of a regulator switch that you would find to control fan speed in the older days. It is a rotating dial-like device that allows you to set the output according to your requirement.
- **Sketches** – Sketches are the programs that you or any other programmer create. When you are done coding, you upload a sketch to your connected Arduino device and then see the results in real-time.
- **Breadboard** – Two things to note here. One, there is no connection between a breadboard with a bread. With that out of the way, the second and more important thing to note is the fact that we use these before finalizing a circuit. These are just like circuit boards, only with so many connections. These are used for prototyping a circuit to see which design works. Once sorted, that design can then be transferred to a real circuit. Without breadboards, there is no Arduino.
- **Shields** – Should you feel like adding more to the project, you call upon Shields. These are additional components that you add to your circuit board, allowing you to do more without actually creating more circuitry. We will see some examples later on.

That about wraps up everything there is to know about the fundamental concepts. If any of the above information seems frightening, I want to reassure you that everything will become clear quickly. We will go through a lot of exercises, all of which have been created to assist you in consolidating your understanding of those challenging ideas and improve your confidence so that you can do more on your own. Arduino is a veritable treasure trove; the more you use it, the more ideas you will get as a result of using it. The first step on our trip is to gain knowledge of where Arduino originated, why we needed it, and how it has gone on to assist a significant number of programmers worldwide. Next, we are going to go into the shopping list, and I am going to speak about and write down everything that you need to acquire to get started. Following that, we will get our hands dirty with some code and dig right in. It will be enjoyable, and there is no doubt that it will be rewarding.

I do not anticipate that you will complete this book in a single sitting. That isn't reading the book for any reason other than the book itself. I want you to take your time and ensure that you completely comprehend every chapter and exercise. Repeat the process many times to ensure that you can properly comprehend what it is that you are doing. If you feel at a standstill, it is strongly recommended that you take a break, maybe have a cup of coffee, and then switch gears and do something else until you are ready to study again. You are acquiring a new language, even if it is not often spoken by people today. Be patient since it will take some time and practice to get the hang of it.

Now that that's out of the way, it's time for us to finally get started with the book and begin delving into the history of Arduino. Prepare yourself to learn about this stunning language packed with incredibly unique ideas that has brought a soul back into this world of mindlessness. Please accept my warmest welcome to the Arduino club!

Chapter 1: Arduino – What on Earth Is It?

The proliferation of internet-based opportunities has resulted in the opening of a floodgate. With each new day that passes, an increasing number of individuals aim to acquire skills that they may later put to use on the internet to create websites, programs, applications, and a wide variety of other things. People that are interested in gaining new knowledge or watching intriguing content online are another type of user. Never before has there been such a seamless flow of information.

Not so long ago, when we saw an integrated circuit, also known as an IC, we were the type of individuals who would think to ourselves, "There is nothing helpful there." We would dispose of it in the trash and go on. Things are different now, especially after the whole pandemic scenario, which prompted these changes. Everyone began participating in various hobbies. Those who decided to venture into the field of programming found that they began to pay attention to details that they would have otherwise ignored. Now, the exact same IC appears to pique our interest in a way that makes us curious. Keeping those ICs for later could be a good idea taking into consideration that we are going to be learning Arduino.

Technology is a race that has eaten some of the most intriguing brains on the planet, and it has kept them occupied in the process of doing so. Something fresh appears every day, astounding all of us and providing motivation to creative thinkers all around the world. Technology never ceases to amaze us, yet at the same time, it never stops making our lives more convenient. Take this book, for instance, as an illustration. If you had told someone thirty years ago that you could read novels on a gadget that you could carry in your pocket, they would have thought you were crazy. However, that is exactly what is possible today because of technological advancements. Now, here we are in the present day.

The Arduino comes to mind at this point. In response to a pressing inquiry, the answer is that it has been available for quite some time now. We were just never informed of its name or the function it served. Because more and more people are getting familiar with Arduino, it is rapidly becoming the platform of choice for novice computer programmers and those who are just beginning their programming careers. For those that are eager to take things to the next level, it not only makes for an enjoyable pastime but also presents fantastic opportunities for professional paths.

Despite all of that being quite intriguing, there is just one issue to which we need an answer, and that is "What precisely is Arduino?"

Let's get to the bottom of it straight away, shall we?

Where Did Arduino Come from?

Allow me to give you a heads-up before I get into the history of Arduino, which is not very convoluted. It's important to remember that Arduino is more than simply a programming language. Please give me a break on this one.

In 2005, the world was introduced to what was, in all intents and purposes, the first Arduino board. It was brand-new, it was intriguing, and students had developed it at the Interactive Design Institute (somewhere in Ivera, Italy). These students started out with the intention of creating a project that would get them a decent grade. In the end, they created a pastime that instantly appeals to the general public. Talk about luck, huh?

At this point, Arduino is a brand name that is well-known and well-respected. Since the concept was conceived in Italy first, it only makes sense for the company's headquarters to be located there as well. It has evolved into a development board with open-source software that makes use of microcontrollers. I am unaware of any other programming language or physical component that has stimulated such a high degree of inventiveness as Arduino, and there are several compelling explanations for why this is the case. Hernando Barragan, the man who conceived of that undertaking, deserves all the credit for its successful completion.

His thesis was titled "Arduino - the revolution of Open Hardware," and he submitted it as part of his degree requirements. It goes without saying that the original title was written in Italian; this is only a translation. Despite the title being a little overly optimistic, it nonetheless managed to carve out a whole new segment in the fields of computer programming and technology. He had presented the world with a brand-new field to work in, one that would welcome participation from individuals of all ages, including children.

This project that Mr. Barragan was working on was a collaborative effort between a total of five different developers. The plan was to develop an entirely original foundation for the wiring. The ones that came before them were notoriously difficult to use and had a high rate of failure. After this was accomplished, they immediately began trying to reduce the cost of acquiring this new piece of technological equipment. They were aware of the opportunities that had presented themselves, and at this point, they desired to cash in on those opportunities. What is the reply? It is impossible for me to argue that it had no effect since it swept the entire world by storm. To suggest otherwise would be a lie. However, Massimo Banzi and a few others went on to become a founder of Arduino - the exact same company that we all know and love. Mr. Barragan's primary concentration was on this wiring platform. In the future, Arduino will employ Mr. Barragan's expertise to develop game-changing new circuit boards for a wide variety of microcontrollers. Because of the overwhelming demand for these circuit boards, they are now known as Arduinos due to their brand name. The firm known as Arduino was making money by selling its own Arduino boards. We shall shortly meet a couple of them and introduce ourselves to them.

Eliminating the Noise

Arduino isn't just known for the insane creativity it brings to the table, but it is known for eliminating the need to learn all the complicated binary coding and many other things.

You see, if you were back in the older days and tasked to program a microcontroller, you'd have your work cut out for you. You would need to know a million different things just to be able to program one. It wasn't easy, and hundreds or even thousands of hours were often wasted because someone forgot to put in the correct value.

When Arduino stepped in, it changed the game completely. Arduino would handle that for you no longer need to learn binary coding. Then, you no longer needed specialized hardware that you would normally use to connect your microcontroller and upload programs. Now, you had simpler breadboards. I can go on and on about what Arduino did, but that would go on for quite a while. In short, Arduino made lives for us programmers a lot easier.

They gave the world their own software, the IDE I mentioned earlier. It works seamlessly across Mac, Linux, and Windows. Then, you don't need to have a specialized degree either. Anyone could pick up Arduino devices and boards, log on to their websites and learn. Of course, their teaching methods involved using the typical cryptic language you would come across in other programming environments. This was a bit of a challenge for those who had never programmed before. This is why I decided to write this book and simplify things for all.

Mr. Banzi, the founder of Arduino, named the company after a frequently visited bar. It was named to honor the place and to honor those who would regularly go there. Not as important, perhaps, but worth knowing in case someone asks you where the name came from.

For those who may be wondering how Mr. Banzi went on to do what he did, he was an associate professor hired by IDII in 2002. He was the one who was working with "Physical Computing." Back then, Arduino was nowhere to be seen since it never even existed. This meant he had to rely on what was called BASIC Stamp. For those unfamiliar with that, it was a microcontroller that Parallax developed. Back then, it was the go-to choice for those working on physical computing. While it was popular among the engineering community, it did come with certain limitations.

There were mainly two problems, and these particularly annoyed Mr. Banzi.

1. BASIC Stamp was extremely expensive for someone like him
2. While it had some computing power, it wasn't enough to help users power bigger projects.

To give you an idea, the board alone would set you back by a whopping $100, with some basic parts. Slice it any way you like; it is still expensive. Then, there was the fact that these boards did not support MacOS, and this was a problem. You see, most designers were using Mac systems, and this was clearly a big no-no. This is where Arduino came to the rescue.

The brains behind the thesis, Mr. Barragan, happened to be Mr. Banzi's student. First, he created software that was familiar to designers around the world. This was called "Wiring." This software came with a good circuit board to go out of the box. This was the foundation upon which the rest of the Arduino empire was built. The idea was ready. Mr. Banzi just worked on it to make it more affordable using the much popular open-source community, and boy, did it work!

It was in 2005 that the first working prototype board was developed. Of course, it wasn't named Arduino right away, but the work was done. The name followed a year later, and the world now had something new, cool, and creative at its disposal. The software for Arduino also became an open-source project. This allowed almost anyone to be part of the project and collaborate. Who wouldn't want to mention "I worked on Project Arduino" on their resumes? Not so fast, though.

When it comes to the open-source model, you generally deal with software – This was hardware and software. First, they had to arrange the necessary licenses, which they did. They opted to go for a license from the prestigious Creative Commons, a non-profit group that normally dealt with music and writing. It was Banzi's idea that a piece of hardware represents a piece of culture and that it should be shared with the world. It worked, and they had their license.

Next, it was the monumental task of lowering the cost. Their idea was to sell the board at $30 each. This was a price bracket that most students could easily afford. Next, they went on to change the color of the board itself. Normally, you would find green boards, but they chose blue – Just a way to stand out from the rest. Unlike other manufacturers, they included input and output pins to make things more interesting. This was a game changer for everyone. As a result, they ended up with a board unlike any other that the world had seen before. It looked more like a home project and invited everyone to learn it.

A test run was carried out, and around 300 blank boards were given to the students at IDII. The idea was to test the functionality of the board and see if it was working for the student community. The goal was to use the internet to understand assembly instructions and then build their unique versions of the board. The turnout was incredible. Hundreds of innovative projects poured in. Arduino had struck a chord, and now the students wanted more.

Seeing the popularity of these boards, the final step was taken, and Arduino was officially listed as a business that produces Arduino boards.

So, Who Uses Arduino?

I will be honest here – Anyone can use Arduino. You can be a beginner, a programmer, a hobbyist, an engineer, or even a seasoned developer. Arduino has something for everyone out there. The fact that kids are using Arduino these days speaks volumes. There are so many projects to work on and limitless possibilities, and it keeps growing. Professionals use Arduino for their ventures, and it is also a great hobby for those who are willing to learn something new, something more creative. Besides, it is the perfect way to learn how to hardwire things, create complex projects, and learn how to code. Arduino has a library full of information that is available online as well as many YouTube videos and courses that teach new Arduino projects every now and then.

Of course, it was initially released for a completely different audience, teachers and students in particular, but with time, it has evolved into something bigger. Arduino is used as a low-cost alternative to building many projects and scientific instruments. As time went on, YouTube came along. When there is YouTube, there are YouTubers, and they have something to look forward to. If you look up Arduino projects on YouTube, you will come across hundreds of thousands of videos, all showcasing unique ideas and projects.

Then, there are those who are working on miniature models of projects that these engineers and developers would one day like to scale up. Instead of working with extremely expensive equipment, they prefer using Arduino boards to help them work on their foundational ideas and then use that to work on larger-scale projects. In fact, musicians have also been using Arduino devices to create new instruments, and it works very well too.

In short, you are only limited by your own imagination, and Arduino offers the simplicity and power to bring those imaginations to life. There is no specific niche here to worry about either. If you love the idea of creating something, Arduino is your go-to option.

The Advantages

There are 6 primary advantages that you have when you use Arduino. These are:

1. The small price tag it comes with
2. Universal IDE – You may have Windows or MacOS, and you can still download and install Arduino's IDE directly from their official website www.arduino.cc
3. It's open-source – This means that whatever code you enter is accessible and readable by others. Before you start panicking, this is actually good news. You see, the open-source community is always willing to help new learners walk the rope. If you ever find yourself stuck, just ask them a question on one of their platforms, and you'll have an answer.
4. Since it is open-source, it also means that the tools are extendable. You can use C++ libraries or AVR-C coding language to further expand your options. Of course, you would need to know a significant deal of programming in order to do that, but it is nice to know that you can always look into this.
5. The Arduino IDE is easy to use, and it is easy on your system. It does not require a great deal of power or computing power. Even your old laptop should run this smoothly.
6. Finally, for those willing to work a little deeper and create their own unique designs, you can! That's the beauty of having open-source hardware. You can easily create your own Arduino board with your color scheme, add-ons, and design, and you wouldn't have to worry about copyright issues, as long as you do not use the same logo (Duh!).

With that said, it is now time for us to dive a little deeper and learn a few important aspects that we will need before we start coding.

Chapter 2: The Key to Understanding Arduino

Let's quickly recap all that we have learned. We have learned the theory behind what Arduino is and what it is capable of. Now, I know that many of you are looking forward to getting started and having a crack at Arduino. That's all good, but you may want to contain that excitement just for a bit. Before constructing a building, you must lay a solid foundation, which is usually the most boring bit. However, I am confident you are willing to learn all you need to, just so you can get started.

In the world of programming, there are phrases and terminologies that we programmers must be aware of. Yes, you read it right – You're on your way to becoming a programmer yourself. However, between then and now, we must walk the path all programmers must go through and learn the basics.

The first and foremost challenge is understanding the terminologies of a given language. Every language comes with some of these, and Arduino is no exception to that rule. The sooner we learn these, the better we will understand what's going on. This is why I see many people buying the wrong boards or downloading the wrong software, then scratching their heads, wondering what went wrong.

Don't worry. While the terminologies may sound complex, they are pretty easy to understand. Arduino is meant to simplify life, and it truly does that. We will be working with an Arduino board, the physical computer board, and coding in the official IDE. The codes that we write are nothing more than instructions that the IDE then compiles, translates into binary code, transfers to the computer on our board (the microcontroller), and then does what we ask it to do. Each of the instructions we write in code is called tools – something you may want to remember.

Okay, time to get to the bottom of this chapter once and for all and get to the exciting bit that everyone is waiting for.

Understanding What You See

For this section, we will primarily be focusing on the board itself. After all, there are so many pins and slots to worry about. A beginner would never understand what's going on, which can often lead to many problems. To help you ensure that these are used properly, let's walk you through each one of these step by step.

The board has quite a few parts. First, we have the digital pins that can be found at the edges of almost every Arduino microcontroller out there. These are used for a variety of purposes, such as:

1. Inputs
2. Sensing conditions
3. Outputs

These exchange information back and forth, allowing the actual microcontroller to understand what's going on and what it needs to do next. Each of these pins is marked from 0, and they usually go to 13. Some boards are bigger in size, in which case the number may go higher. For our demonstration, we are using the Arduino UNO – A classical choice for beginners and professionals alike.

When it comes to your inputs and outputs, you will use these every time you use the board. These are used to provide input commands and acquire results. It's quite simple, really. Let's say that the input instruction is to dim the light intensity. The output would then follow suit and ensure that the light is dimmed as per instructions from the input. See how this works?

Most boards generally come with a pin named LED. This is a special pin that can often be found right next to pin number 13. The LED pin is used for debugging purposes to find the problem and fix it. It is also dedicated to helping you with the first built-in project called "Blink Sketch." Don't worry, we will cover that later on.

Speaking of the 13 pins, you may also find the word "digital" just on top of a solid white line. Don't worry about that now. You will also see some of the pins have a tilde sign "~" next to numbers. These pins have access to special features, some of which we will explore later in the book.

Moving forward, we have the obvious one – The power LED. If the Arduino board is switched on, the LED lights up. However, you can also find it useful during debugging sessions.

Now, you might notice that big, black block on top of the board. That's the brain where all the operations take place. That's the microcontroller, the heart, and soul of the Arduino board. We call this ATmega microcontroller. Without it, you have a board that doesn't know what to do. It is like a human being without a mind – a Zombie with no purpose.

You will see something called "Analog In" pins on the other side of the board. These are input pins that provide you access to the Arduino system. Since it says analog, it means that the signal transmitted back and forth is not constant. It continues to vary with time. Think about audio input that continues to fluctuate in volume and intensity.

See how it says "GND" and 5V on the next pins? These allow you to connect additional power of up to 5V to the circuit and the microcontroller. Furthermore, the GND stands for ground, meaning that you can use that to ground your circuits.

Moving forward, we have the power connector. It is usually on the very edge of your Arduino board. We use this to supply power to the microcontroller when your board is not connected to any computer via its USB port. Obviously, you can always use the USB as a power source, but a USB's main function is to transmit data back and forth, allowing you to upload sketches and instructions to your board or receive information from the board. However, you will not need USB power for most projects to keep the Arduino microcontroller on. Once the sketch is uploaded, you just hook it up with a supplementary power source, and that's it.

Next, we have the TX and RX LEDs. TX and RX indicate active communication between your computer and your Arduino board. Whenever you are transmitting data, these lights will flicker on and off rapidly, indicating that your machines are talking to each other. Best not interrupt that.

After that, we have our USB port. This one is pretty self-explanatory. You connect your Arduino board with a computer and upload sketches or download real-time information from other pins that may be receiving or sending data. You can also use the USB connection to power your Arduino board, just in case you run out of additional power. Well, all we are left now is that little RESET button. Press that, and it resets everything, including the microcontroller, all the way back to its factory settings. Any information that you have uploaded it's gone now!

That's the entire Arduino board, or is it? We will come across quite a few things, but these are essentially all the things you need to know about the board.

Also Good to Know

Arduinos come with three types of memories. Memory is nothing more than a space where we store information, such as the sketches we upload. When required, these are recalled by the microcontroller so that the program can function. It works just like our minds. We meet hundreds of people in our lives and store some information about them. Years later, when we meet them, we recall that specific piece of information, such as name, and we carry on with the conversation, hoping that we got the name right.

We start with something called a flash memory. The flash memory is used for storing all your programs. We programmers also refer to it as the "program space," something you may want to remember. Whenever you upload a new program or a new sketch, this part of the memory is used automatically, so you don't have to worry about typing in specific commands that tell the system which memory to use. Flash memory does not lose its data when you disconnect Arduino from the computer or turn its power off. It remains in the flash storage until it is removed or overwritten.

Then, we have the second type of memory, which is called SRAM. You might have already guessed this one, and you'd be correct. You see, the SRAM stands for Static Random-Access Memory. Where the programs you create and upload into your Arduino get stored in the flash memory, the inputs and results your programs create are stored in the SRAM. Unlike the flash memory, this type of memory is temporary, meaning that the instance you turn the Arduino off, this memory is wiped clean – It's like a goldfish!

The third and final type of memory your Arduino boards come with is called the EEPROM. Don't blame me; I'm just explaining here. Whoever came up with these acronyms really needs to work on them. Anyways, the EEPROM stands for Electrically Erasable Programmable Read-Only Memory (try saying that super-fast).

The EEPROM is like your miniature hard drive that stores information other than the sketches or the programs when your Arduino is switched off. You might imagine, "Why would it do that?" However, there are things that happen even in a closed computer, which is why it is able to know exactly what time it is the next time you turn it on. To access EEPROM, you need to use specific instructions to read, write, or erase information. There are other functions that EEPROM offers, but they are a little out there, so we won't be covering those here.

Moving forward from the memory, there are some other things you need to familiarize yourself with before you jump into the greasy and cryptic world of coding. There are certain pins, digital pins to be precise, that are designated as PWM pins. These Pulse Width Modulation pins allow you to create analog results using digital means. Remember those modulating pulses and frequencies displayed on the old amplifiers with green lines that would change with a twist of a knob? That's essentially what you are looking at.

Digital pins generally create a constant flow and do not modulate or vary. Using the PWM pins, you can create "pulses" of energy varying from 0 volts to 5 volts in strength. There will be some projects where you will need to use these, so it is a good idea to know what they are capable of doing.

When we talk about computers, we talk about their processing speed. Since our Arduino boards come with microcontrollers, it is worth knowing what speeds they offer. Don't get too excited; you won't be gaming with these any time soon! We use the term "clock speed" to measure the processing speed at which our microcontroller works. The more the speed, the faster it will process. However, don't look for the fastest Arduino board available because the more powerful it is, the more power it will consume.

Next, you might come across a serial port named UART. These are used to establish smooth communication between your Arduino board and computer using serial communicational lines. If you are short on processing power, these lines will help you overcome the lack of power as they transfer data serially as opposed to parallel or simultaneously. Serial data transfers are always easy on the power consumption and don't require a great deal of power. The only downside is that you will have to attach more physical wires, which may not look eye-catching.

You can also use your Arduino boards to connect to the Internet of Things (IoT) devices besides your own laptop or desktop computer. It would allow you to transmit data back and forth to numerous things that may be interconnected, allowing you to have meaningful outputs or results. These may be a bit advanced, so we will not cover these in this book.

Okay. We have learned the theories, what Arduino is, where it came from, and what it can do. Now it is time for us to get started for real this time. With that said, grab a pen and paper, and let's shop Arduino!

"Wait, what?"

Well, you weren't expecting to learn Arduino programming without an Arduino board, were you?

"Umm… No!"

Great! Let's go then.

Chapter 3: Know Your Choices

Well, congratulations. You are now about to start your journey into the world of endless possibilities and creativity. However, between then and now stands a tough question – Which Arduino should you start with?

It is a tough question that has often baffled most newcomers and learners. However, I am here to help and guide you through the selection. The idea is to understand what a specific board offers and why it is good or bad. At the end of it all, I will tell you which board I recommend. While you are free to choose your own board if you like, it is still a safer bet to start with the one I recommend. This is because it will be easier for you to know which pins I am referring to or what part of the board I am talking about. I don't want you to be stuck with a board with a high processing speed and only 5 pins, whereas we are talking about connecting something to pin 13, and you are wondering, "What do I do now?" It has happened to me, which is why I want to ensure it doesn't happen to you. Okay. Time to get started!

The Crazy World of Arduinos

I will list some of the most useful and famous Arduino boards first, followed by the entire line up. However, before deciding which board you want, you might want to check online on Amazon or at Arduino's website to see if specific models are available. At the time of writing this book, some models may be available, but by the time you read it, they might have been replaced or discontinued. Therefore, I take no responsibility if a certain piece of equipment is no longer available.

UNO

This is the finest board money can buy. It is small, sturdy, and exceptionally reliable. It is the go-to choice for all professionals and beginners. It is common practice for all beginners to start their Arduino journey with Arduino UNO.

Right away, it isn't the fastest or the one brimming with the most feature. It is definitely not the most compact one either, yet it sits right in that sweet spot of perfection. It isn't needlessly complicated and offers many features, almost every single one we will discuss in this book. Furthermore, this is the one I will be using for this book.

It doesn't cost a fortune, but you can easily see why. It tends to have the smaller processing power and smaller memory. However, it makes up in functionality where it lacks in power. It comes with a mini-USB port, allowing you to upload your programs and sketches to the board without the use of a breakout board or any additional add-ons. Here are the stats and figures that may interest you to give you a full overview.

Oh, and a quick note. The prices that you see here are taken straight from Arduino's own website. Once again, these may change from the time of writing to the time of reading. Be sure to check these before you make a purchase.

Model: UNO R3
SRAM: 2kB
Flash Memory: 32kB
EEPROM: 1kB
Input Voltage: 7-12V
Operating Voltage: 5V
Processing Speed: 16MHz
PWM Pins: 6 pins
Digital Pins: 14 pins
Analog In: 6 pins
Price: $27.60

Leonardo

If Arduino UNO is small, wait till you see this one. Leonardo happens to be a beast of a board with a powerful microcontroller. Fully functional from the get-go, it is a great board to have for bigger, more complex projects. Connect a micro-USD cable, and you're in business. To make things a little more interesting, your computer will recognize this board as a keyboard or a mouse, thanks to the ATmega32U4 processor that it comes with. You get a little more pins than the UNO R3, and you have yourself some increased capacity for workload management. All in all, it's a good one to start with as well.

Model: Leonardo
SRAM: 2.5kB
Flash Memory: 32kB

EEPROM: 1kB
Input Voltage: 7-12V
Operating Voltage: 5V
Processing Speed: 16MHz
PWM Pins: 7 pins
Digital Pins: 20 pins
Analog In: 12 pins
Price: $24.90

Nano

Next, we have the wonderful Nano model. As the name implies, it is small… I mean a lot smaller. Don't be fooled by the size, though, because it can still get things done nicely. While it is one of the smallest boards Arduino produces, it is still a great board for your projects. The board is capable of linking itself to a breadboard, just like UNO R3 and Leonardo, but it does have a little downside. The Nano does not offer you any DC power jack. The only way to power this tiny thing is to use a mini-B USB cable, and that may often be tricky to get.

Model: Nano
SRAM: 2kB
Flash Memory: 32kB
EEPROM: 1kB
Input Voltage: 7-12V
Operating Voltage: 5V
Processing Speed: 16MHz
PWM Pins: 6 pins
Digital Pins: 22 pins
Analog In: 8 pins
Price: $24.90

Micro

If Nano is too small, you might want to look at Micro. The Arduino Micro board is somewhat bigger than Nano but still relatively smaller than Leonardo and UNO R3. Once again, this device will be recognized by your system as a mouse or a keyboard, thanks to the built-in USB port. While it may be somewhat similar to Leonardo, there are quite a few differences for you to consider.

You see, Micro was developed with Adafruit, which happens to be yet another company that creates Arduino shields and other products. You get a good number of output and digital pins, a reset button, an impressive 16 MHz crystal oscillator, and some other cool features. Overall, it is still a good choice if you do not prefer the UNO R3.

Model: Micro
SRAM: 2.5kB
Flash Memory: 32kB
EEPROM: 1kB
Input Voltage: 7-12V
Operating Voltage: 5V
Processing Speed: 16MHz
PWM Pins: 7 pins
Digital Pins: 20 pins
Analog In: 12 pins

Price: $24.90
Mega 2560 Rev 3
Okay, this is where things get bigger, I mean a lot bigger. The Mega 2560 Rev 3 is an 8-bit board. It offers you a whopping 54 digital pins, 16 analog inputs, and four serial ports. Talk about an impressive start, eh?

Mind you, you might not want to jump on the internet right away. You see, this one is particularly designed to handle larger projects. This is the one for you if you are into robotics or 3D printers. However, if you are just beginning, you may want to skip this one. While you get significantly greater space, it is worth noting that this board is used for programs with many instructions.

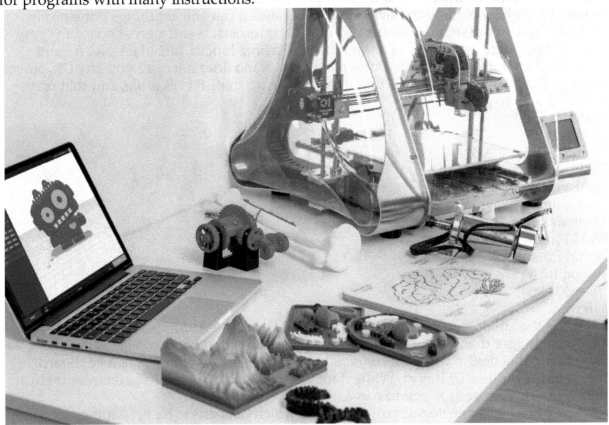

Model: Mega 2560 Rev 3
SRAM: 8kB
Flash Memory: 256kB
EEPROM: 4kB
Input Voltage: 7-12V
Operating Voltage: 5V
Processing Speed: 16MHz
PWM Pins: 15 pins
Digital Pins: 54 pins
Analog In: 16 pins
Price: $48.40
Zero

You might be wondering, "How can Zero be a good sign," right? Well, don't worry. This actually happens to come with quite a few enhanced features. You have a powerful 32-bit extension of the very same platform that UNO uses. Then, there is the increased performance, thanks to the incredibly increased processing speed, and not to forget a high flash memory. While the extensions will cost you twice as much as a regular UNO R3, it is worth the price because you end up effectively doubling your hardware capabilities.

Then, there is its built-in feature called Atmel's Embedded Debugger, more commonly known as EDBG. This means that you don't have to debug your code anymore; Zero will do it for you.

Model: Zero
SRAM: 32kB
Flash Memory: 256kB
EEPROM: n/a
Input Voltage: 7-12V
Operating Voltage: 3.3V
Processing Speed: 48MHz
PWM Pins: All except 2 and 7
Digital Pins: 20 pins
Analog In: 6 pins
Analog Out: 1 pin
USB port: 2 micro-USB ports
UART: 2 lines
Price: $47.40

Due

This is the first-ever Arduino board that is based on a 32-bit ARM core microcontroller. It is considered a novelty in the world of microcontroller boards.

The Due comes with a great deal of power, an exceptionally fast processor, 4 UART lines, and so much more. This brings a lot of flexibility for developers and allows for large scale Arduino projects to be carried out swiftly and smoothly. While it is a wonderful thing, it isn't exactly ideal for being your first board.

Model: Due
SRAM: 96kB
Flash Memory: 512kB
EEPROM: n/a
Input Voltage: 7-12V
Operating Voltage: 3.3V
Processing Speed: 84MHz
PWM Pins: 12 pins
Digital Pins: 54 pins
Analog In: 12 pins
Analog Out: 2 pins
UART: 4 lines
Price: $48.40

Nano Every

If you are looking for the cheapest board you can find, look no further. The Nano Every is designed to cater to the needs of those who may be on a tighter budget or for those who just want to see what the fuss is all about. Therefore, if you want to try this one out first, just to get the feel of things, it is a good choice.

Since it is arguably the smallest of the lot here, it is recommended to most users who are looking for boards that are easy to use. People use this board to create wearable projects, electronic musical instruments, tiny robots, and so on.

Now, you might imagine that the smallest one wouldn't exactly pack a punch, but you'd be wrong. In fact, it offers you 50% more power than UNO. The ram is also jacked up by 200%, so you won't be running out of that any time soon.

Model: Nano Every
SRAM: 6kB
Flash Memory: 48kB
EEPROM: 256 bytes
Operating Voltage: 5V
Processing Speed: 16MHz
PWM Pins: 5 pins
Digital Pins: n/a
Analog In: 8 pins
LED Built-in: 13
UART: 1 Line
Price: $11.10
Nano 33 BLE (Without Headers)

Make room for yet another tiny but impressive board on the table. The Nano 33 BLE comes with a low energy Bluetooth and an inertial embedded sensor. Of all the boards I have picked out so far, none of them come with these two features as standard, and that is what makes this really special.

Now, before you go on to buy this, I would still say this isn't exactly a beginner-friendly one out there. This board is specifically meant for experienced developers looking to create wearable inventions or working on projects that have short-distance communication. Even that might not be problematic, but when it comes to soldering, that is where we step back. You don't want to start with a board where you are constantly soldering things, only to find out, "Oh, I meant pin 2!"

Model: Nano 33 BLE
SRAM: 256kB
Flash Memory: 1MB
EEPROM: n/a
Input Voltage: 21V (limit)
Operating Voltage: 3.3V
Processing Speed: 64MHz
PWM Pins: All pins
Digital Pins: 14 pins
Analog In: 8 pins
Price: $24.30

Nano 33 BLE Sense

The Nano 33 BLE Sense is an upgraded model of the Nano 33 BLE. What this board does is add the power of artificial intelligence – Yes! You read that right. Not only are you going to love the power the Nano 33 BLE brings, but you are now getting to add AI to all your projects. The board comes pre-loaded with sensors, allowing you to "Sense" multiple things (See what I did there?). These sensors are:

- 9-axis inertial sensor – This makes your board an ideal choice for wearable devices, allowing for 9-axis movement tracking.
- Temperature sensors
- Humidity sensors
- Light intensity sensors
- Gesture sensors
- Light color sensor
- Light intensity sensor
- A microphone to capture audio
- Barometric sensors

That's quite a line-up, don't you think? But wait, before you rush, again, know that this isn't a beginner-friendly board. You may want to mark this one down for later, but don't start with this one right away.

Model: Nano 33 BLE Sense
SRAM: 256kB
Flash Memory: 1MB
EEPROM: n/a
Input Voltage: 21V (limit)
Operating Voltage: 3.3V
Processing Speed: 64MHz

PWM Pins: All pins
Digital Pins: 14 pins
Analog In: 8 pins
Price: $27.60

Arduino Starter Kit

Ah, yes! If all of this has confused you, bewildered you, baffled you (you get the point), Arduino has something for you that just might tickle your fancy. Instead of taking chances, you can settle for Arduino's very own starter kit. Now you might think, "I'm not too sure if I will get much out of a starter kit," but wait till you see the line-up of things you will get if you choose to settle for a starter kit. Ready?

- One Arduino Uno
- One USB Cable
- Project Book (170 pages of awesome goodness)
- One breadboard (has 400 points to connect with)
- 70 solid core jumper wires
- One easy-to-assemble wooden base
- One 9V battery snap
- One stranded jumper wire (black)
- One stranded jumper wire (red)
- Six phototransistors
- Three potentiometers (10k Ohms)
- 10 push buttons
- One temperature sensor
- One tilt sensor
- One Alpha-numeric LCD
- One LED (bright white)
- One LED (RGB)
- Eight LEDs (Red)
- Eight LEDs (yellow)
- Eight LEDs (green)
- Three LEDs (blue)
- One small DC motor 6/9V
- One small servo motor
- One piezo capsule
- One H-bridge motor driver
- One Octocoupler
- Two Mosfet transistors
- Five capacitors (100uF)
- Five Diodes
- Three transparent gels (green, red, blue)
- One male pins strip
- 20 resistors (220 ohms)
- Five resistors (1 kOhms)
- Five resistors (4.7 kOhms)
- 20 resistors (10 kOhms)
- Five resistors (1 MOhms)
- Five resistors (10 MOhms)

Wow! That actually hurt my fingers typing all that. Do you see what I mean here? You are essentially getting a ton of toys to play with.

"What about the price?"

Ah! Well, the price is a pocket-easy one: **$110.30**

That's what you call a bargain! If you were to buy these components individually, you'd be spending a lot more than that.

Other Board Worth Knowing

Well, you already have a significant line-up to choose from. However, should you still feel like you want more, you can always browse to www.arduino.cc and look at their impressive line-up. They keep updating or adding new ones every now and then. Besides, other brands do the same thing, such as Adafruit. That's the beauty of open-source hardware; anyone can pick one up and redesign it.

You can check Amazon, eBay, and all the other relevant places to find someone selling Arduino boards near you, just in case they are out of stock on Arduino's own website. Just remember, you need to focus on a model that is beginner's friendly. You don't want to jump into something more complicated if you don't intend to continue with Arduino for more than just a few projects.

With that said, it is time for us to dive into some other models that are worth looking at. You can use this list to pick one that interests you now or maybe after learning how to code in Arduino.

M0

At the time of writing, this model appears to be retired. However, this board is still available through private sellers. You can also search other brands and manufacturers to find eligible replacements for this model. You will still get the exact same design and functionality, but it would be from a different brand.

Originally, the M0 was designed to serve as an extension to UNO R3. By connecting the two, you would end up getting the 32-bit power of the renowned ARM Cortex M0 Core. The board was a major hit with people because it offered added functionality and immense power to your usual UNO R3 board. These were used for wearable inventions and robots and were also a good choice for projects involving the Internet of Things.

Model: M0
SRAM: 32kB
Flash Memory: 256kB
Input Voltage: 5-15V
Operating Voltage: 3.3V
Processing Speed: 48MHz
PWM Pins: 12 pins
Digital Pins: 20 pins
Analog In: 6 pins
Price: $30.00 (Prices will be different from seller to seller)

M0 Pro

If M0 wasn't powerful enough, you could pick up M0 Pro. It came with some extra functionality, a good debugger (EDGB), and a good processing power. This was a little on the higher end in terms of price, but it was worth every penny that was invested.

Model: M0 Pro
SRAM: 32kB
Flash Memory: 256kB
Input Voltage: 5-15V
Operating Voltage: 3.3V

Processing Speed: 48MHz
PWM Pins: 12 pins
Digital Pins: 20 pins
Analog In: 6 pins
Price: $55.99 (Check prices before purchasing)

Arduino YUN

The Arduino Yun is certainly one of the greats, especially if you are trying to connect to the Internet of Things. If you are trying to design a device connected to a network, this is the board to go for. Having a built-in Ethernet port, it allows you to have a blazing fast internet connection along with a reliable Wi-Fi module that allows you to connect your board with wireless networks.

However, this device, as it turns out, is listed as "retired." This means that they may not be producing this at Arduino.cc, but you may still be able to find one elsewhere.

Model: Yun
SRAM: 2.5kB
Flash Memory: 32kB
EEPROM: 1kB
Input Voltage: 5V
Operating Voltage: 5V
Processing Speed: 16MHz
PWM Pins: 7 pins
Digital Pins: 20 pins
Analog In: 12 pins
Price: At the time of writing this book, the best price I was able to find was around $80.00.

Arduino Ethernet

Unlike the above, this one only comes with an Ethernet port. However, it is still no pushover. It is based on the ATmega328 microcontroller, the one you find in a standard UNO R3. This means you get a decent processing power along with many connecting options. The pins from 10 to 13 are reserved for Ethernet interactions, which is why this board may not offer that many pins. This can be a problem for those who need to have more devices connected.

The good thing, however, is that this board comes with a built-in Micro-SD card slot, allowing you to expand your storage options significantly. Furthermore, it uses an FTDI USD cable to upload or download sketches. You can also use an FTDI breakout board, which is an extension that can be connected to the board.

I know, this one is a lot more complicated than the rest, which is why it isn't the ideal choice for those starting their Arduino journey. However, it is still a good board overall.

Model: Ethernet
SRAM: 2kB
Flash Memory: 32kB
EEPROM: 1kB
Input Voltage: 7-12V
Operating Voltage: 5V
Processing Speed: 16MHz
PWM Pins: 4 pins
Digital Pins: 14 pins

Analog In: 6 pins
Price: Around $55.00

Tian

The Arduino Tian isn't exactly what you call a board. It is more of a miniature computer at best. It has a built-in microprocessor on top of its microcontroller. Again, complicated, but bear with me on this one.

The Arduino Yun offers both wireless internet connectivity and Ethernet connectivity. Having both means you would have to pay a higher price, but for that, you get better functionality and power.

The process, however, is in a league of its own. It is blazing fast, clocking at speeds of about 560 MHz. It also comes standard with Bluetooth capabilities, allowing you to use its functionality in short-distance projects, such as robots or sensors. However, using this board is a bit of a tricky business. It uses Linino OS, which is a flavor (variant) of the renowned Linux operating system as well as OpenWRT.

Model: Tian
SRAM: 32kB (+64MB DDR2 RAM from its microprocessor)
Flash Memory: 256kB (+16MB flash memory from its microprocessor and 4GB eMMC from the same microprocessor)
Input Voltage: 5V
Operating Voltage: 3.3V
Processing Speed: 48MHz (+560 MHz from the microprocessor)
PWM Pins: 12 pins
Analog In: 6 pins
Price: $110.00 (check price)

Industrial 101

As the name implies, this is more of an industrial option. However, it is essentially a trimmed down version of the Yun, and for half the price. The Industrial 101 was designed to be used with long-standing projects, which is why it would be a good pick for those who may want to work on something that is a little more permanent or long-term natured project.

It comes with both Ethernet connectivity and Wi-Fi, as well as a USB connection port.
Model: Industrial 101
SRAM: 2.5kB
Flash Memory: 16MB (processor)
EEPROM: 1kB
Input Voltage: 5V
Operating Voltage: 3.3V
Processing Speed: 16MHz (400 on the processor)
PWM Pins: 7 pins
Digital Pins: 20 pins
Analog In: 12 pins
Price: $55.00 (Check price)

Leonardo ETH

The Arduino knew it was doing great with Leonardo. However, who wouldn't want to have additional connectivity features on something that was already brilliant? Of course, everyone did, and everyone welcomed Arduino's Leonardo ETH.

This particular variant of the already famous Leonardo line-up came with an Ethernet port, allowing all users to connect their projects to IoT devices and networks. Furthermore, the same port could be used to have internet access, further allowing greater control over sensors. It also meant that a user was now able to use their device as a server to transmit information back and forth.

The Leonardo ETH also came with Micro-USB port, allowing for easy communication between the board and the computer. You no longer need a breakout board or some kind of a TKDI cable (trust me; you don't want to search that).

To make things even more interesting, you had the option of increasing the storage capacity as this one also featured a micro-SD card reader. I wouldn't be wrong to say – This was Leonardo on steroids… The board, I mean.

Model: Leonardo ETH
SRAM: 2.5kB
Flash Memory: 32kB (4kB reserved for bootloader)
Input Voltage: 7-12V
Operating Voltage: 5V
Processing Speed: 16MHz
PWM Pins: 7 pins
Digital Pins: 20 pins
Analog In: 12 pins
Price: $60.00 (Check price)

The Gemma

Arduino has been involved with Adafruit for quite some time now. Together, they have produced some incredible tech together. One of them came in the form of Arduino Gemma. It is a miniature board designed to work with wearable projects. It is perfectly circular, hence why it was such a hit with people working on wearable projects.

Since this was a small board, it needed very little space on your workstation. The Gemma came with a micro-USB connection, which was somewhat new since boards of this size usually previously required breakout boards. Now, that was no longer an issue. You were good to go by connecting the board directly to your computer.

Model: Gemma
SRAM: 512 bytes
Flash Memory: 8kB
EEPROM: 512 bytes
Input Voltage: 4-16V
Operating Voltage: 3.3V
Processing Speed: 8MHz
PWM Pins: 2 pins
Digital Pins: 3 pins
Analog In: 1 pins
Price: $15.00 (Check price)

Lilypad USB

This is yet another round, circular, cute little board that can come in really handy. It is based on the ATmega32u4 microcontroller by Arduino, giving you a decent processing power. With a Micro-USB connection, you don't need breakout boards here either. Furthermore, it came with a JST connector that allowed you to connect any 3.7 lithium polymer battery, in case you didn't want to power your device with USB cables.

There is something worth noting here. Lilypad is a long line-up of miniature boards. If you look closely, you will find both Lilypad Arduino and Lilypad Arduino USB. The only major difference here is that this one comes with a Micro-USB connectivity whereas the regular one doesn't. If you opt for the regular one, you will need to pay a little less at first, but then you will need to buy breakout boards to compensate for the lack of connectivity.

Just like the gemma, this is also aimed at developers working on wearable projects. You can easily sew this in cloth, leather, or any other fabric of your choice.

Model: Lilypad USB
SRAM: 2.5kB
Flash Memory: 32kB
EEPROM: 1 kB
Input Voltage: 3.8-5V
Operating Voltage: 3.3V
Processing Speed: 8MHz
PWM Pins: 4 pins
Digital Pins: 9 pins
Analog In: 4 pins
Price: $35.00 (Check price)

Lilypad Main Board

Yet another one in the wearable Arduino board line-up. Just like the Lilypad earlier, this too can be sewn into any piece of fabric with great ease. You can also pair this up with sensors of your choice as well as actuators and power supplies.

The Lilypad Main Board does have a drawback though; you need a breakout board for this. If that wasn't bad, you also need to acquire a TKDI cable in order to connect this board to your computer. This is perhaps why this was an inexpensive entry, but then again, it does deliver good results.

You can try SparkFun.com to find good prices on these, along with several other boards.

Model: Lilypad Main Board
SRAM: 1kB
Flash Memory: 16kB (2 kb Is used by the bootloader itself)
EEPROM: 512 bytes
Input Voltage: 2.7-5.5V
Operating Voltage: 2.7-5.5V
Processing Speed: 8MHz
PWM Pins: 6 pins
Digital Pins: 14 pins
Analog In: 6 pins
Price: $20.00 (Check price)

Time to Shop

Okay, that was quite an extension list, but hopefully, it was able to provide you with significant information. If you are still confused about which board you should settle for, take the safer approach and aim for an Arduino Starter Kit. It is loaded with a lot of goodies and will keep you busy for a very long time. Furthermore, it helps save you the trouble of ordering a board and then realizing, "I need all the other stuff too!"

The boards that I have shared with you in this chapter are meant to highlight some of the finest that have come out. However, this does not mean that these were the only ones worth looking into. Arduino and many other companies continue to push out newer boards with newer technologies, which is why I always encourage fellow programmers and developers to keep an eye out for these.

Time now to let you do your bit of the work and shop for your first ever Arduino kit. It is exciting, it is incredible, and it is something that will really help you find a new hobby that is worth pursuing.

Next, we will move towards understanding what makes a board good, and we will also look into how to set up the environment properly.

Chapter 4: Pick, Buy, and Set Up Your Arduino

I am sure you might have already browsed through Arduino.cc, the official website for Arduino. It is also possible that you might have also gone through some other websites, such as Adafruit and SparkFun if you have already ordered your Arduino, great job! If you are still unsure for some reason, you might find this chapter helpful to help you make a sound decision.

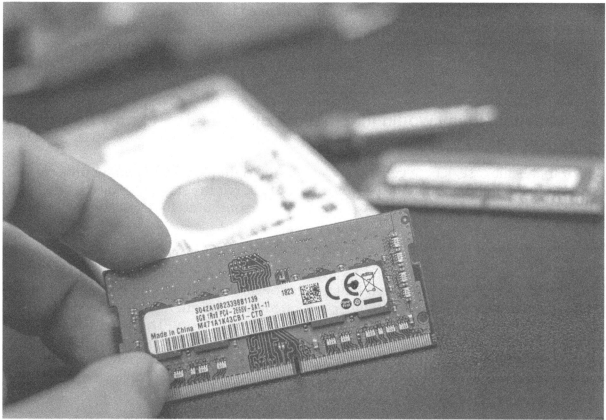

Not only will this chapter help you find the right board that truly fits your requirements, but it will also dive into setting up the working environment.

Side Note: Since I am using a MacOS Monterey on an M1 Chip, the installation process we will look at later might differ from yours.

Know Which Board Is Right for You

The previous chapter might have given you loads of ideas and a lot of excitement. However, just because a board has so much to offer or is apparently the best does not mean it is the one to go for. Depending on your preferences, such as frequency of use, how complex your projects will be, and how many features you truly need, your board choice may vary. This is why the Arduino community always chooses the Arduino UNO R3 as their first board. It is a perfectly balanced board that offers significant connectivity, good processing power, robustness, and creative prowess.

With that said, there are a few questions you will need in order to understand what you want and which board truly suits you. These questions will help you make the right decision and probably save yourself from a lot of hassle and trouble, maybe some money too.

I have an idea I would like to work on, but I don't know how much power I need

Well, if that is the case, let me get you started on the right foot. The first few projects you are going to do aren't going to be power-thirsty at all. For the starting projects, any board will work flawlessly. However, there is a general rule of thumb that you should remember:

The more complicated the project, the more power it needs!

Let's say you want to work on a night bulb that changes color all night. It isn't too complicated, and it should not need that much power at all. However, if you want to create a robotic arm with many moving components and torque, you will need a board with higher SRAM, processing power, and higher flash memory. This is why if you browse through YouTube, you will see many projects using many boards at the same time. Essentially, they are connecting multiple headers or extension boards with the main board to provide such an output.

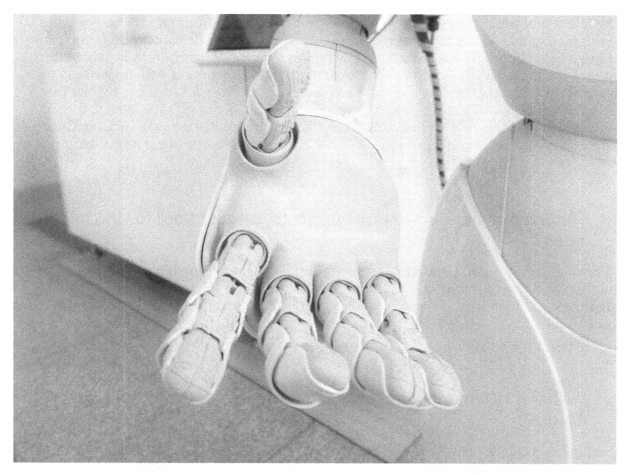

For starters, however, the Arduino UNO should be just fine. In fact, it has enough capability to handle most projects of small to medium complexity. Once you have mastered your way around the board and understood how things work, you can then upgrade to things like Arduino Leonardo, Mega, or something similarly powerful in nature.

What's with the pins? How many should I be targeting to acquire enough functionality?

This is pretty similar to the above. Since you will be working on beginner projects, you will not need many pins to worry about. While I encourage you to work on projects using multiple connections, the starting ones are a lot easier. The idea is to understand how to use these pins, how to differentiate between them, and learn what they can actually do. Without knowing, you cannot decide if you want boards with more pins or less.

The initial few projects that we will cover in this book would not require you to use a lot of digital pins or PWMs. However, once you have learned your way around, you can upgrade your board to one that offers a wide range of pins. The more complex your project, the more pins it would need. However, be sure to know if you are looking for more PWM pins or Analog or digital. Each one of them functions differently and offers different results.

Your Arduino UNO, whether you buy it separately or get the one that a starter kit comes with, has a sufficient number of pins. You won't be running out of connectivity any time soon.

I am interested in wearable projects. Should I opt for the miniature ones?

That's a good question. However, if you are certain that you wish to seek something on the wearable side of things, it's not a bad idea to order one. However, I would still suggest ordering this in addition to your starting kit or Arduino UNO R3. This is because some of the projects we will learn in this book may not function properly in these miniature models.

What If I Want to Connect My Arduino Project with the Internet of Things?

The previous chapter gave you a perfect picture of which of these are worth buying if IoT is your field. You will need a board that gives you Wi-Fi capabilities, Ethernet functionality, and maybe Bluetooth as well. Depending on how much power you need, you can pick one up that suits you best.

Remember, this will be much more advanced than the usual boards, and we will not be covering IoT-related projects in this book. The scope of this book is to stick to the basics and focus only on projects that can teach us how to use Arduino boards and the IDE.

Well, I hope that you were able to find an answer and were able to buy yourself a board. If you are waiting for your board, it is probably a good idea to set up your computer by downloading Arduino's official IDE.

Downloading the IDE

Downloading your IDE is actually quite simple. You need nothing more than to visit Arduino.cc. Once the website loads, you need to click on "SOFTWARE" which should be right at the top, next to "HARDWARE."

On the next page, you will see your download options. At the time of writing, the latest version available was Arduino IDE 1.8.19. Yours might be different, but it is exactly the same thing.

Now, depending on your operating system, choose the right variant from the options to your right. Since I am using MacOS, I will be downloading the Mac OS version of the software.

When you download, the IDE zip file will be downloaded to your system. This is the same for all OS users. For Windows users, simply extract the content and run Setup. Follow the prompt, and you should be done in no time.

For MacOS users, once the file is downloaded, open the file and double click on the Arduino icon. The IDE should start almost immediately.

That's pretty much it. No tampering with settings or doing anything needlessly complicated. Now, all you need is to wait for your board to arrive. Once it does, it is time to connect your board via a USB cable to your system and start with the first program.

Side note: If you see a little prompt in the bottom left corner that says "Update to some libraries available," go ahead and click on that to install all available updates. You will need to be connected to the internet in order to download these. They aren't that big and should be done fairly quickly.

My First Program

Finally! We are now in the techy territory that most of us have been waiting for. I do apologize for stretching it out all the way, but had I not done that, most of this information would have never made sense to you. You'll know why soon.

Go ahead and open up your Arduino IDE. It looks crisp, simple, a bit cryptic, and elegant. You will soon get used to seeing all that, and almost everything you see there should start making sense by the time you are done with the first few projects.

Let's look at what we can see in our IDE. You should be able to see something that says the following:

```
void setup() {
// put your setup code here, to run once:

}

void loop() {
// put your main code here, to run repeatedly:

}
```

The above two are pretty much self-explanatory, but to ensure you get the concepts right, let me quickly explain.

You see, all the code we write must be between the curly braces. This is why you see the open curly braces after the void setup() and void loop(). The first one, which is the void setup(), is where we type in the code we want our board to run once. Think about it as more of a thing you do when you start something. You only need to do it once.

The next one, void loop() is where we enter our main code. This is intended to run repeatedly until the Arduino board is powered off or runs out of battery.

Don't worry about the setup() and loop() functions for now. We will learn what these are later on.

Uploading Your First Sketch

It isn't as simple as connecting a USB cable from your board to your computer. Unfortunately, there is something that must be done here in order to make your Arduino talk to your computer.

You see, in order for you to upload any sketch to your board, you must direct your computer to use the right port and the right board. Every Arduino board comes with its own settings. Fortunately, we don't have to do much except set a few things right.

While things have changed, allowing you to just connect your device and use it, if it doesn't work, follow the steps.

For Windows users, when you connect your Arduino board, you should be able to see what COM port the board is attached to. If you see it, you don't really need to do much. However, if it doesn't, you will need to choose the right board.

1. Go to Tools
2. Click on Port
3. Choose the model of your board that applies

Once the right port is connected, we then move towards uploading our very first sketch to the board. I know what you are thinking. You haven't written anything yet, how can you possibly upload a sketch? Well, your IDE comes with some pre-built sketches for you to use.

It doesn't matter what operating system you may be using, you all get these pre-loaded sketches with your IDE copy. These are designed to help you learn more about Arduino programming and can often be a great way to see if your board is connected properly and working.

Each of these sketches provides you with significant information about how they are coded, what to expect, and steps to follow. For now, we will stick with our basic pre-loaded sketch called Blink. To access that, go to File, Basics, and click on "Blink."

Once you click on this, you will see a new window open, but this time, this window will have a bunch of code written in there. It is exactly like the one you saw at the start of this book.

Your code should look like this:

```
void setup() {

pinMode(LED_BUILTIN, OUTPUT);
}


void loop() {
digitalWrite(LED_BUILTIN, HIGH); // turn the LED on (HIGH is the voltage level)
delay(1000); // wait for a second
digitalWrite(LED_BUILTIN, LOW); // turn the LED off by making the voltage LOW
delay(1000); // wait for a second
}
```

The first part, which is written in grey font, is a comment. It is to facilitate other programmers and learners to understand what's going on. These are instructions for you to understand and follow.

The actual program itself starts with the usual void setup() { part. I haven't changed any part of this code, so it should be exactly the same.

This sketch essentially makes your board blink a connected LED light on and off. Depending on how high or low the number is within the delay() parameter (value that goes between the parenthesis), the light will behave differently.

For clarification, 1,000 milliseconds mean 1 complete second. If you leave it at default, the light will blink for a second and then turn off for another second. You can toy around with these numbers to create a different light show of your own.

You don't really have to change any values if you do not want to. Some go ahead and upload this sketch to your connected Arduino board and watch what happens.

"But how?"

Oh, yes. I forgot. To upload a sketch, you simply need to click on the "Upload" action button. This is a circular button right next to the check mark that stands for "Verify." It's as simple as that.

Now, here's a thing or two worth noticing. The instance you press that upload button, a few things will happen. You will notice that the RX and the TX lights will start going berserk. This is an indication that the board is both transmitting and receiving data.

"Hey board. I have something for you!"

"Oh really? What is it computer?"

"Here's a new sketch… Get cracking!"

Next, you will also notice a progress bar just beneath the code window. This just lets you know how much of the sketch is uploaded or how much of it still remains. Since we are dealing with a basic sketch, it should literally take no more than a second to upload.

After the sketch is done uploading, the TX and the RX LEDs should stop blinking. This is an indication that there is no more communication between the computer and the board. However, the LED at pin 13 will start to blink. If you haven't changed anything in the code above, this LED will blink for one second and then turn off for the following second. This will be played out in a loop over and over until you power the Arduino board off or hit that reset button.

Great. You've uploaded your first sketch, and you have seen it in action… sort of. Now, we are going to tweak a few numbers here and there in the same sketch. The idea is to play around with the values to create a kind of a light blinking pattern we like and find fancy.

Head on over to the void loop() part. Any code that goes between the curly braces is called a block of code. We will be modifying an already existing code to make it more… interesting!

We will use both the digitalWrite(LED_BUILTIN, HIGH) and the digitalWrite(LED_BUILTIN, LOW) and change their values.

The digitalWrite is a function that we call upon. A function is essentially a pre-made block of code. Every function that we call upon is represented by a name, followed by open and close parenthesis, hence digitalWrite(). Between these parentheses, we use attributes or parameters that we pass through this function. In the above cases, we are passing LED_BUILTIN to notify that we want this function to use the built-in LED that comes with the board, and then we are passing the value HIGH, which directs the function to pass a higher voltage. Similarly, we are using the LOW value to indicate we want the built-in LED to be turned off.

HIGH = ON

LOW = OFF

"Ah! Now it makes some sense."

You see? It wasn't that complicated, was it? If I was to interpret the code above in simpler terms it would literally sound something like this:

"Hey, computer. I want you to digitally write (read modify) the state of the built-in LED and turn it on for 1,000 milliseconds, and then I want you to turn it off for 1,000 milliseconds. Do this over and over again."

Time to change the values. Instead of using 1,000 milliseconds, reduce the HIGH delay to 500 milliseconds, and do the same for the LOW delay as well. Now, the LED will blink on and off twice as fast. You can alter values to your liking freely. If you are afraid this would burn your board, rest assured; it won't.

With that said, you have successfully uploaded your first sketch, and you have learned how to modify values without burning your board out. Easy, exciting, but still a bit basic. That's about to change, though.

Before diving into more technicalities, it is probably a good idea to understand every piece of code, comment, and all you will be using. We will be looking at a variety of things, all of which we will use when we create our own sketches or programs. It will also help you understand a lot of the programming world as well, allowing you to learn more programming languages in the future.

Chapter 5: Coding 101

For this chapter to truly work its magic, I want you to read this chapter with pen and paper. If you like, you can also use your smartphone or laptop to take notes. This chapter is where things will get a lot more technical.

In order to truly harness the power of Arduino, we must know how to use it right. This means we will look at why we are using a semi-colon ";" at the end of a coded line. We will learn why it is written as digitalWrite and not DigitalWrite or digitalwrite. We will also look into all the basic components that make a code work properly. Therefore, let's not waste any time and dive right into the coding world.

Understanding the Syntax

Earlier, I mentioned the term "Syntax." A syntax is essentially the structure for any programming language out there. Every programming language comes with its own applicable structure. Arduino is no exception to that rule either, as it too has its own syntax that we must understand and follow. From how to write a code to how to ensure the system knows where a coded line ends, we must learn everything. So, let's start with the two obvious ones.

loop()

It's not Loop; it's "loop." Arduino is a case-sensitive language, meaning that you must enter the name in that specific order if you were to call upon a function, a variable, or any other functionality.

When it comes to loop(), it is essentially a function. Recall how a function has its own pre-made block of code. We will not be looking into what that code is. We are interested in learning what this does and why we use it.

Arduino is a board that takes in a sketch and then is meant to repeat that sketch in a loop, over and over again. However, if you were to write a block of code in setup() instead, that will be carried out once. In the case of the blinking LED sketch, we wanted the LED to continue blinking endlessly until we interrupted the process ourselves.

The loop() is one of the two basic functions that you get whenever you load up Arduino's IDE. Whatever goes in here simply repeats itself over and over, provided that the code you have entered is correct.

setup()

Once again, setup() is a case-sensitive function. If you were to replace setup with "Setup," the compiler will not identify what you are talking about and will render an error in the process.

This function is where you put in something that you want the system to do as soon as you load the sketch on the Arduino board. Let's say you want to write a sketch where you are going to measure the temperature. In order for you to get correct readings, you want to ensure that the temperature sensor is first set to 0 so that it starts afresh.

Alternatively, you may have a program where you are going to use some kind of a push button to count the number of pushes. If your program starts and the counter starts at 311, you will not be able to record the correct data. You first need to reset the counter to zero and start the process. In such cases, you use the setup() function to carry out a few things right at the start.

The Control Structures

Now that you have a decent idea of what setup() and loop() do, it is time to take things up a notch. Let's assume that you want to create a sketch that is able to make a decision based on the situation it is presented with itself. This is where you will need control structures. In simpler words, this is where you create a smart program.

So far, we have only seen the blinking light example, and that wasn't exactly smart in any way, shape, or form. This is because the code itself was rather simple and did not use any control structures. Now, if you were to change things a bit and introduce some controlling elements, that simple light show could become something better, something smarter.

By using control structures, you add conditions to the program. When these conditions are met, you tell the computer what to do. For example, let's assume that you wish to create a program that measures temperature. However, you want your program to take decisions based on these scenarios:

1. If the temperature exceeds a certain point, record the temperature and turn the fan on.

2. If the temperature drops below a certain point, record the temperature and turn the heating on.
3. If there is no change in temperature, wait for a while to see if any changes occur.
4. If nothing happens for a certain period of time, turn the system off.

If you code this right, you will be able to create a program that can take decisions based on the scenarios it presents. This is a very theoretical but good example of how smart programming works and how control structures can help you do that.

If you happen to be a gamer, you may have noticed how you get an additional life if you collect 100 rings or coins in some games. Similarly, if you were to lose all of your lives, the game over sign appears, and the game stops. Then, there are the checkpoints which, if activated or crossed, will save your progress and allow you to resume from the last checkpoint. All of this is smart programming. All of this is done through the use of control structures. With each situation, the program checks to see if any of the described condition is true. If it is, the code block residing under that condition will be carried out. If not, it will move on to the next condition and the next until it either meets a condition. If all conditions are false, it will carry out an alternative action.

To help us create something similar, we use one or more of the following in our sketches:

if

We use the "if" keyword to tell the compiler that we want it to check for a certain condition. The "if" is essentially a conditional statement where we specify what condition the system or the program must check. It literally translates to "If this is true, then do this." We can use multi-colored LEDs to see how this works. If a condition we describe is true, we would want the green LED to light up.
"But what if a condition isn't true? Would that crash the program?"
Not really. That is because whenever we use **else.**

if...else

The "if" part is the first condition. If that is met, the green LED will light up. However, should the condition be false, or not met, we would want the system to do something "else."
if A > B, light up the green LED... else, light up the red LED!
That is literally how it works. We will see this in greater detail and use it for some of the programs I have lined up for you.

switch case

This is yet another conditional statement. However, unlike if and else, where you have a single condition for each, we use the "switch case" if we have multiple conditions we want the system to check. Each of these conditions will have their own unique variables and their values.
You use switch case when you want your program to check for these values and make decisions based on those values. Therefore, if a player has 100 coins, add one life and reset the counter to zero. If the player has 99 coins and is hit, reset the counter to 60 and add no additional life. That's essentially how the switch case works. Depending on how the player is performing, the system will then carry out the decisions for you.

for

We use "for" as a loop statement. A loop statement is essentially a loop that will continue to run and increase or decrease values. Let's say you want to run a loop where a number continues to increase by one every single time it runs. To do that, we use the "for" loop.

while

As shown above, the "while" is yet another loop statement. However, unlike the above, this loop only continues to run for as long as the defined condition is met. Let's say you want a loop to count how many times a number is pushed, and you want the program to increase the value by one for every single push of a button. However, you want it to ensure that it stops counting as soon as the count reaches 100. Once that happens, the count will not register any additional button pushes.

The "while" statement always checks the condition first and then executes itself. This is an important bit to remember.

do...while

This tends to work almost the same way as the "while" loop, but the only major difference here is that it first "does" something, meaning it executes the block of code first and then checks to see if the condition is true. If it is, it will execute itself again, check the condition until that condition is no longer true. This, therefore, is a loop that will run at least once and then check the condition. The "while" loop may run, and it may not run at all if the condition is never met.

break

Handling loops can often be tricky, especially if you are a beginner. The problem is that if we use a loop, it just goes on forever and ever. It just doesn't stop. Let's say you want a loop that displays the number "1" on the screen and then adds one for every single loop that takes place, it will just keep doing that forever. Given the speed at which the processor works, you would have an error or a number too large to fit the screen in a matter of seconds, and it will continue generating error. That's a problem.

To help us with that, Arduino has an emergency "break" statement that serves as an automatic "panic" button. We generally use the break keyword when we aren't too sure if a loop will work fine. This is particularly true for loops that have conditions or nested conditions within them. You don't want to find out how bad it can be when a condition is always true, meaning that the code just keeps executing itself over and over again, with no end in sight. By putting the term "break" at the end, it tells the system, "Dude! Do this once and snap out of it."

continue

We use continue to skip an iteration and let the rest of the loop continue.

return

Okay, this may sound a little scary, but bear with me. By using the keyword return, you terminate a function that is currently ongoing, return a value from any given function to what is called a calling function. Sounds like a handful, doesn't it? Don't worry. You will learn this better through practical experiences.

goto

If you are a C programmer, you may think, "Oh No! We don't use that." You're right. We generally don't recommend using the goto, but just for reference, we use goto to instruct the microcontroller to move to another labeled point. I won't get into the technicalities here as that will take things to a very advanced level.

Understanding the Syntax

Now that we know these keywords, it is time to learn how to write your code correctly.

The Semi-Colon ";"

Old timers would know what a terminator is. Every language has it, and Arduino does as well. The semi-colon is used to effectively terminate a line of code. Just like we use the "full stop" or "period" at the end of an English sentence, we use the semi-colon to let the computer know where a line of code ends. However, not every line comes with a semi-colon. If you look through the code that was loaded up on Arduino's IDE for the blink sequence, you will see that the terminator was used in some places, but not all. There are two exceptions:

1. If a code you are typing ends with a curly brace, use the semi-color before the closing curly braces.
2. If you are typing comments, the ones that are greyed out, you do not need to use semi-colons at all.

These are the only two exceptions. Otherwise, every line and every instruction must end with a semi-colon.

//

The double forward slash are used to indicate single-line comments. Comments can be whatever you want them to be. These are proper sentences written down by programmers to instruct other programmers what a piece of code does. This is why you will see so many of the sketches and programs having comments.

By using the //, the IDE immediately knows, "Okay! I am not supposed to compute this." It literally skips over this. Whatever your comment may be, it won't count or be computed as long as you use a // at the start of a comment.

/* and */

Single-line comments are good, but what if you want to type in comments that are stretching more than a single line? That's where you use the /* and */ to type in multiple lines of comments.

/* This part indicates the start of the comment. I can type in whatever I want to after this. I can then continue doing that until I feel like the comment is sufficient. Once sure, I will then end the multi-line comment with */.

The above is literally a multi-line comment. If you copy and paste that into your Arduino IDE, you will see how all of the text above is written in grey fonts.

Single-line comments and multi-line comments have one more effective use. Consider this as a pro tip. If you have a line or a block of code that you do not want the computer to compute, simply use the appropriate comment command, and those lines will be greyed out. It helps save time and allows you to do things quicker. Also, you may have some code that you want to keep there, just in case you ever need to use it. In such cases, you can convert all of that block as a comment, and then remove the comment commands when you feel you need to use that block of code.

{} The Curly Braces

Functions use simple braces we call parentheses. The curly braces are used for advanced and somewhat more complex operations. These are generally used when defining conditions, controlling structures, and loops, or writing down big blocks of code to define or create functions.

When using these braces, be sure to type both the opening and the closing braces first. You can then move your cursor in the middle of these two and hit enter a few times to give you enough space to write your code. Quite often, people forget to type in a closing brace, which is why their programs may crash. Without a closing brace, the computer would not know where your block of code or function ends, and this can cause problems.

#define

C++ programmers, anyone? You would know what this is. The #define is derived from the C++ language. By using #define, you gain the ability to set a specific name to any kind of constant value you intend to you before the program is compiled by the compiler. A constant that is defined does not consume memory space, and this can often be quite helpful, especially if you are working with smaller devices that have little space. Here's a quick example:

#define ledPin 4

//Here, #define does not need a semi-colon, so we won't be using a terminator.

#include

Arduino uses libraries from external sources in order to access multiple features and functionalities. There are some functions that may be called upon only if you have the relevant library available and under use.

You see, Arduino does not use all these libraries automatically, nor is it able to know which library to load if you are calling a specific function. You need to specify categorically which library or libraries it should use. To do that, we use #include as our keyword.

To give you an example, we have a library called "LibraryFile.h" and we use that quite often. To load that library, we will need to type the following:

#include <LibraryFile.h>

// Once again, we will not be using a semi-colon here either.

When you gain access to libraries, you gain access to a lot more features and functionalities. You can learn all about different libraries, what they do, and when they can be used right at Arduino's official website for free. For now, let's focus on yet another important piece of the puzzle – operators.

Chapter 6: The Arduino Operators

Operators are essentially your symbols, such as +, -, /, and so on. These are used to carry out a variety of functions and operations. They are also great to use with conditional statements and loops as they will help you design more efficient and precise programs.

The Arduino operators are divided into a few types, each specifically catering to a field of operation. Let's dive in and understand how to use these operators and what they stand for.

The Arithmetic Operators

Most of you might have guessed by the +, -, and the / symbols that operators use for arithmetic operations. True, but that's not all they do.

Every programming language uses the same set of operators to carry out arithmetic operations. This simply means that if you learn the arithmetic operators for Arduino, you would easily be able to understand and use these in any other programming language.

The Assignment Operator (=)

Now I know what you are thinking, "That's an equal to sign." Well, you are right if you are doing mathematics on a piece of paper. When it comes to the programming world, things change a little.

In any programming language, the equals to, or the = symbol, is called the assignment operator. Let me explain using the following piece of code:

Int number = 101;

The above is a simple demonstration of how the assignment operator works. You see, the assignment operator assigns the value on the right to the variable on the left. Therefore, if you run the code above, the variable "number" will now be assigned a value of 101. The reason we don't term this as an equal to sign is because variables continue changing values.

int number = 101;
int number = 102;
int number = 103;

In the above, the variable remains the same. However, each line the compiler compiles will assign the latest value to our variable. In this case, it will first assign 101, then 102, and finally 103. You will not be able to recall previous values if your variable has already been updated.

For those who are wondering what the "int" stands for, it simply means integer. You will need to define what kind of data goes into a variable. In this case, the variable "number" is a variable that will hold an integer value. That value is the one assigned from the right side of the assignment operator.

Addition

This one is pretty universal. Just like how you would use a calculator and use the + sign to add things up, we do the same in programming. When you are trying to add two variables together, you use the addition operator, or the + sign, to carry out the operation.

There is, however, a catch here. If you were adding two variables with the same datatype, such as integers, you will be able to do that easily. However, if one of the variables is an integer and the other one a string (which is a fancier way of saying text), it will not compute and return you with an error.

There is another thing worth knowing here. You cannot add a big number with another big number that easily. You see, since we are dealing with very small memory space, these variables have certain limitations. If the resulting number is greater than the maximum value your variable datatype can hold, you may end up receiving a negative number. If that happens, don't panic. It simply means you need to use a different datatype to store a larger number.

Subtraction

Once again, subtraction does exactly the same thing as you would expect. Just like addition, we also use the same universally-accepted symbol of the minus sign (-). The same limitations apply here as well, just like they did for additions.

Division

Now this is where things will change once again. Generally, we are used to seeing the division sign as ÷, but in the world of programming, the division operator is represented by a single forward slash, or /. Don't confuse this with the double forward slash because that stands for a single-line comment.

Modulo

Ah, yes. This one is quite different. In fact, I am sure many of you may have never even heard of this. The module operator is essentially a percentage sign of %. This lets you know what the remainder would be if you were to divide two numbers together. For example, if you were to divide 10 with 4, you would end up with a remainder of 2. This is because the number 4 cannot perfectly divide 10. Instead of using the divide sign, simply use the % sign, and you're good to go.

The Comparison Operators

The above were operators you should know for all your arithmetic needs. Next, we have the comparison operators. These are more interesting in nature and will require some practice to fully get the hang of things.

The comparison operators are great to know because they help you compare values, create better conditions, and come up with desired outputs more effectively. Remember the smart programming? This is where the magic happens.

The Equal To

I was saving this for now. You asked earlier why the = sign was not an equal to sign. Well, now's the time to reveal the reason why that is the case.

You see, the equal to sign isn't =. In fact, it is == or double the usual sign. We use the equal to operator to create conditions. For example, if the temperature is equal to 90 degrees, we would like the fan to turn on automatically. In this condition, we will use the variable's name, the equal to operator, and a value of 90.

The equal to operator is used when you want a perfect match. This means that if the temperature is 89 or 91, the condition would still remain false. It will only work when the temperature is 90.

The Not Equal To

Not everything is meant to be equal. There may be instances where you may have certain conditions running in the background, creating all sorts of output. Then, you may want to find an anomaly, and to do that, you will use the name of a variable you wish to trace, use the not equal to operator, and the subsequent value. Whenever something falls out of line, this condition will be met and whatever block of code or instructions you wrote down will be carried out.

The not equal to operator is denoted by !=. That's an exclamation mark followed by an assignment operator.

Greater Than

This one is pretty standard and easy to use. Like in mathematics, we use the > symbol as our greater than operator in programming languages. We use the greater than symbol to create conditions for both the control structures and the while/do…while loops.

Lesser Than

This is also the same as you would expect to find in your regular mathematic textbooks. You use the < symbol as the lesser than operator. You are then able to create conditions that help you compare values, something that you will be doing quite a lot soon.

<= and the >=

Where there is greater than, there is also greater than or equal to. Similarly, we also have the lesser than or equal to operator.

The greater than or equal to operator is represented by a greater than symbol followed by the assignment operator, making it look like >=. The lesser than or equal to is the opposite, meaning it looks like this <=. These are great when you aren't too sure if the value would be lesser than or equal to a number, or perhaps larger than or equal to a specified number.

Constants

You need them, you'll like them, and they are super handy at times. These are expressions that are pre-defined in nature. We use constants to make programming easier for us to read and for everyone to understand. Constants are classified in a few groups. Let's walk through each of these.

Logical Level

Have you ever heard of something called a Bool or a Boolean value? Almost every programming language has these and they are datatypes that we use to define something as true or false.

A Boolean variable can only ever hold one of the two values; TRUE or FALSE. If something returns as zero, it is considered as False. Anything that isn't a zero, the program would identify as True.

These are written in all-uppercases. Therefore, if you are trying to declare a variable or use a bool value of TRUE in a condition, you need to type TRUE as opposed to "true" or "True."

The PIN Levels

Remember the HIGH and the LOW? That's essentially what we will be looking at here. If you are trying to read something or write something using a digital pin, you only ever get two values you can use. These are either LOW or HIGH.

Understanding LOW is a lot easier, but HIGH is where things get a bit tricky. It takes a bit of messing around for you to understand how to properly use it. The behavior will vary depending on the pin you are using, whether you are using it as INPUT or OUTPUT.

If you are using a pin as an INPUT, which you can do using the pinMode(), and the pin is set to read, using digitalRead(), your Arduino IDE will report HIGH when one of the two happens:

1. Pin has a voltage that is greater than 2.0V (for boards with 3.3V operating voltage)
2. Pin has a voltage that is higher than 3.0V (for boards that have an operating voltage of 5V)

You can always configure a pin to work as an INPUT pin by passing the pin number through the pinMode() function. You can then change it to HIGH using the digitalWrite() function. With that said, if you have your pin set as an OUTPUT, using the pinMode() function, and you have used digitalWrite() to pass HIGH as its parameter, the pin will hold maximum voltage.

1. For boards having an operating voltage of 3.3V, the pin will have 3.3V
2. For boards having an operating voltage of 5V, the pin will have the same

Using pinMode() is something you will be doing a lot. You will be using various pins and setting some of them to act as INPUT while others to work as OUTPUT. You can then use the digitalWrite() function to change voltage from LOW to HIGH, just like we did in the first example for the blinking LED sketch.

For pins with LOW settings, your Arduino would report a pin as LOW if:
1. The pin holds a voltage lesser than 1.5v (for 5V boards)
2. The pin holds a voltage lesser than 1.0V (for 3.3V boards)

There is one exception to this rule. If you have set your pin to work as an OUTPUT, and you then set the pin to LOW using the digitalWrite() function, your pin will have 0V on any board. This is something that often confuses a lot of beginners, which is why you may always want to check this part first before assuming that your board has gone bust.

The Digital Pin Modes

Your digital pins have modes which can be accessed using the pinMode() pre-defined function. We use this function to change the digital pin mode to:
- INPUT
- OUTPUT
- INPUT_PULLUP

Every change that your digital pin undergoes will change the electrical behavior of said pin.

If you are defining a pin as INPUT, the IDE will consider that specific pin to be in "high-impedance" state. What this means is that this particular pin demands very little power. We use this to allow our pin to read sensors more effectively, without worrying about blowing them out.

Your Arduino microcontroller comes with what are called "Internal Pull-Up" resistors. These can easily connect with the power you have on your board internally. If you are not so happy using any external pull-up resistor, you can use these. Just add the INPUT_PULLUP to the pinMode() function, which should do the trick.

With that said, if you connect your pins that are set to INPUT or INPUT_PULLUP with voltages that are lower than the ground voltage, or anything above the positive rail (which is either 5V or 3V, depending on your board), they will blow out. You can learn more about these limitations at Arduino.cc.

With all said and done, the term HIGH doesn't mean it has high voltage, it just means it has a higher impedance state. If you set your pin to act as OUTPUT, it is considered as a pin with a low-impedance state. What this means is that this pin can provide significant current to any other circuit with relevant ease. Of course, it does mean that you should not connect these with ground or positive power rails, as doing so would leave you with a small cloud of smoke and a few final sparks.

The Built-In LED

You might have thought, "Hmmm… It's just an LED that comes as standard." Well, it is that, but it is a little more useful. You see, Arduino boards, most of them, do come with this built-in LED. This is generally connected to some kind of an on-board pin. For most cases, you would generally find it connected to pin 13. Your Arduino UNO R3 has the same setup as well.

In order for us to use this built-in LED, we need to instruct Arduino to do so using LED_BUILTIN. This is why you saw the following in many lines within the IDE.
digitalWrite(LED_BUILTIN, HIGH);

Here, we are instructing that we want to write something using the built-in LED and write (or modify) the value to HIGH.

Well, all that is left now is to learn the datatypes. These are also important because you can't just go around naming variables or assigning them with some values without first declaring the variable properly.

Chapter 7: Understanding the Datatypes

I promise you; you are closer to creating your own programs than you might think. If you do not understand the basics, it would literally make no sense to try and create a sketch or upload one.

You see, every programming language has a use of datatypes. These datatypes define your variables and tell Arduino what kind of values these variables are to hold. When it comes to Arduino, we will be going through the following datatypes:

1. Void
2. Boolean
3. Char
4. Unsigned Char
5. Byte
6. Int
7. Unsigned Int
8. Word
9. Long
10. Unsigned Long
11. Short
12. Float
13. Double

Let's dive straight into it.

Choose Your Datatype

Let's start with the first one – **Void**.
We use void to declare functions. This is to tell the microcontroller that we are not expecting any information to return whenever this particular function is called upon. To give you an example, the setup() function or the loop() function don't really return any information or values back. They just carry these out regardless.

Boolean or Bool

Earlier, I mentioned how Boolean variables can only take one of two possible values; TRUE or FALSE. We use bool values for comparative purposes or to set up conditions for our control structures. When you have more than one condition, you can use both TRUE or FALSE in a variety of ways. You can say:
1. If condition A is TRUE, do this. If Condition B is TRUE, do that. In this case, you will need to use two different statements.
2. If condition A "and" B are TRUE (or FALSE), do this.
3. If condition A is TRUE "or" condition B is FALSE, do this.

These are just one of many combinations, and you can achieve these using the "and" and "or" operators. When you want both the conditions to be TRUE or FALSE, you use the "and" operator, which is &&. If you want one of the two to be either true or false, you use the "or" operator, which is | |.

Char

Char stands for Character, which is essentially a single letter. A char also has numeric value, meaning that you can carry out complex arithmetic operations as well. However, we mostly use Char for character representations in most cases.
If you are trying to create a variable called "myChar," and assign it the value of "A," you will do the following:
char myChar = 'A';
Note how I used a single quotation mark here. This is important to remember. Unlike integers and numbers, you will need to use a single quotation mark if you are trying to store a single letter as a variable. If you are using multiple letters, such as "ABC," you will need to use double quotations marks. Therefore, this is how you would use your Char datatype properly.
char myLetter = 'A';
char myLetters = "ABC";
Unsigned Char
You know now what char stands for and how it is used. But what about an Unsigned Char? Well, this is exactly the same as char, but the only difference is that this uses numbers from 0 to 255 to represent characters. The usual characters are essentially "signed" characters. The unsigned char datatype can also represent negatives as well.
Byte

I will keep this short – Byte is exactly the same as Unsigned Char. It uses numbers from to 255 to represent characters in a 8-bit system. To give you an example, B10010 may be of no significance to you, but it actually represents the number 18. This is binary talk, and we won't be covering that in this book so don't really worry about this.

Int

Whenever you aim to use integer values, which are whole numbers, you use the integer datatype as industry standard practice. Most Arduinos come with a 16-bit system, meaning that the system can store a minimum value of -32,768 all the way to 32,767 for every integer variable. However, if you are using a 16-bit system and you store the number 32,768, you will end up with a negative number, which is to indicate that you exceeded the maximum number available to be stored in an integer variable.

If you are working with slightly more advanced variants of the Arduino boards, you may have options of working on a 32-bit system. If that is the case, you can store a minimum number of -2,147,483,648 to a maximum value of 2,147,483,647. Any values lower or higher than these limits would cause an error.

Unsigned Int

For 8-bit boards, you can use unsigned int to store numbers from 0 to 65,535. Of course, this is an alternative, meaning you always have the option of using integers as opposed to unsigned int. However, since you will be working mostly with 8-bit boards in the start, it is a good idea to use a datatype that allows you to store more values. However, note that with higher value comes higher space on the memory.

The only major difference here is that unsigned integers only cater to positive numbers, not the negative ones.

Word

It's not what you think. Simply put, using Word allows you to store a 16-bit unsigned number on your board. If you are using Due or Zero, you will store a 32-bit number using Word.

Long

If you really want to store a massive number, you opt for the long datatype. Now, you might think that creating a variable to hold a long value would be something like this:

long distance = 1800000;

You would be wrong. To properly declare and store a long variable, you will need to assign the upper-case letter "L" right at the end of the number to let the system know, "Hey! This number is long…"

long distance = 1800000L;

You see, the long datatype allows you to store numbers from -2,147,483,648 to 2,147,483,647, just like the int datatype, but there are some technical differences. It depends on what board you are using, if it is 8-bit, 16-bit or 32-bit, and so on. Should you ever encounter error, try switching to long instead of int and that might solve the problem.

Unsigned Long

If you are trying to find a datatype that allows you to store the largest available number, you go for unsigned long. The unsigned long gives you 4 bytes or 32-bits to play with. Since this datatype is unsigned, you end up accessing numbers from 0 to 4,294,967,295.

Short

You can use short to store integer values between -32,768 to 32,767. The Short is a 16-bit datatype. By using short, you free up space on your boards, especially on Due and Zero. What short does is simply halves the number of bits it uses to store a number, something that can often help you create faster programs without wasting your space.

Float

So far, we have been fixated on whole numbers, but what about decimal numbers? Well, float is a high-precision datatype that allows you to store a number followed by six to seven decimal places. That isn't all, it can help you store pretty large numbers. However, the downside with using floats is that they take up quite a lot of space. They aren't really practical if you are trying to create a big project that needs all the space available.

Double

If you have bought yourself the Arduino Due, this is applicable only to you. Double allows you to double the precision of a float number. For people who have bought themselves the Arduino UNO or any other variant, this may not be something you would be using at all.

The Battle of Cases

Okay, so far, you might have already understood this, but to really hammer the point home, I wanted to highlight one final thing. Arduino is a case-sensitive programming language. You get the cases wrong, and you end up running into errors.

This stands true for variables, functions, datatypes, and every conceivable and usable feature present within the Arduino. Therefore, if you use pinmode() instead of pinMode(), it won't work. It won't work if you use PinMode() either.

Arduino follows a specific naming convention where the first word is always lowercases and the next word that follows always starts with an upper case.

With that said, it is time to get our hands greasy and start cracking some codes.

Chapter 8: Cracking the Code

Okay, it is time to start dissecting some codes. We will begin with the very first one that came forth. I will paste it here again so that you do not have to scroll all the way up. However, to make it more helpful, type the code out as you see in your Arduino's IDE window.

```
const int PinkL = 13;
void setup ()
{ pinMode(PinkL, OUTPUT); }
void loop ()
{digitalWrite(PinkL, HIGH);
 delay (500);
digitalWrite(PinkL, LOW);
delay(500); }
```

With all that you have learned now, you should now be able to make more sense of this code. However, to help the learning process along, let's walk you through line by line.

Right away, the first thing we did was to declare an integer variable, PinkL, and assigned the value of 13 to it. To ensure this value does not change, we used the keyword "const." Recall how variables have the ability to change values. To ensure that doesn't happen, we make this a constant number. Therefore, PinkL will always be assigned a value of 13. Next, we have the familiar line:

```
void setup() {
pinMode(PinkL, OUTPUT);
}
```

I have simplified the format, so don't be alarmed to see the curly braces on top and bottom of the block of code. This is usually how we will be writing our code. It is far cleaner, and it is a lot easier to understand. With that, let's go back to the code.

We learned that if we are using void, it literally means we don't expect any return here. Therefore, the setup() function used would carry out the function without giving us anything in return.

The setup we want is essentially to switch the PinkL (which is currently working on pin 13) to OUTPUT mode. We do that using the pinMode() function. By doing so, Arduino will stop taking data from it and will instead use the pin. Let's move forward.

```
void loop() {
digitalWrite(PinkL, HIGH);
delay(500);
digitalWrite(PinkL, LOW);
delay(500);
}
```

Okay. So void loop() is where the magic happens. Nothing is returned, but whatever the block of code that goes inside the loop() function gets repeated over and over. Here, we are first telling Arduino to change the state of the pin PinkL to HIGH. This means that this pin will now operate with 5V flowing through it. If we use the LOW keyword, it will have 3V flowing through it.

The delay() is a function that takes in numeric values as milliseconds. The higher the value passed through delay(), the longer the operation will be. In this case, we want the light to turn on for 0.5 seconds and we then want it to turn off for the next 0.5 seconds. When you will eventually start using a breadboard and connect your own sets of LEDs, you will need to use this code as a test to see if your LEDs are working. You see, LEDs come with something called polarity. To the untrained eye, the two legs or connectors of the LED will look exactly the same. However, if you put it the other way around, the LED will not work. To ensure the connection is correct, you will need to turn the LED and connect it in the right way so that the positive leg connects to a positive port and the negative terminal connects to the negative port.

Some Tips Worth Remembering

When it comes to the Arduino IDE, where you will be coding a lot, there are a few additional things you will need to know before you are able to program properly. Below are some handy tips and reminders for you.

- All kinds of spaces, such as tabs, white spaces, and blank lines, all of them are perceived as a single space.

- Every parenthesis you use must have a relative opening and closing brace. If you have two open parentheses, you will need two closing parentheses for the program to work properly.
- Every block of code you group must be done using curly braces.
- Do not use commas to represent thousand, million, billion, and so on. If you want to type a million, just type 1000000 instead of 1,000,000.
- Every programmable statement ends with a terminator. The exceptions were already discussed earlier.

There is a great "Reference" section available on Arduino.cc to help you with any piece of code that you find confusing. Be sure to check this often because this may help you save your program, your board, and eventually, your project.

At this point, stop and pat yourself on the back. You have now covered all the basics that go into any kind of sketch. However, we are not here to learn just the basics, are we? In fact, what's the point of mentioning smart programming if we aren't going to learn how to use it? Therefore, brace yourself because we are about to learn the next big thing in Arduino – The Logic Statements!

Chapter 9: What On Earth Are Logic Statements?

When you need an effective way to compare or check values of a given variable with another one, you use logic statements. It is through logic statements that you fully understand what will happen next in any given sketch. You effectively create a smarter program that is able to make decisions based on their current scenario, as long as this scenario was pre-defined by the user.

To help you learn more about logic statements, Arduino has a wonderful sketch that is pre-made for you. Let's load that up, shall we?
1. Go to File
2. Hover over Examples
3. Select "02.Digital"
4. Click on Button

Don't worry if you do not have the IDE right in front of you. Here's how it looks like:

```
// constants won't change
const int buttonPin = 2;
const int ledPin = 13;

// variables will change:
```

```
int buttonState = 0;

void setup() {

 pinMode(ledPin, OUTPUT);
 pinMode(buttonPin, INPUT);
 }

void loop() {

 buttonState = digitalRead(buttonPin);

 if (buttonState == HIGH) {
 // turn LED on:
 digitalWrite(ledPin, HIGH);
 } else {
 // turn LED off:
 digitalWrite(ledPin, LOW);
 }
 }
```

The code is a lot smaller if you take away the comments. These comments are there to help you understand how to set this up and how the rest of the program will work.
I am sure a lot of you might be looking at the code and are able to crack it. Good job nonetheless. This sketch is really easy to understand as you have learned most of the things already.
We see that we are using two constant variables which represent the pin numbers assigned to them. The first one is buttonPin, which is assigned to pin 2, and the other one is ledPin, which is the LED light on pin 13. We don't want these values to change since our push button and our LED will remain where they are.
Next, we have a variable that will change over time. This is the buttonState, and it is initially setup with a value of 0. Remember that we only need to set this value once every time this sketch is loaded and started. This is to ensure that the counter is reset to zero and that any operation carried out is done correctly.
Here's something you might have not yet noticed. These constants and variables have been declared even before we got to the void setup() part. You can do that and it will work. You see, when the program runs, it will first take these values in, create variables accordingly and then move towards the void setup() part.
Next, we have the void setup(). Here, we have set ledPin to act as OUTPUT whereas the buttonPin to act as INPUT. Since we will be pushing that button, we will be providing an input. The LED will then blink on and off, to reflect an output.
Moving further, we have the void loop() block of code. This is where things get different. While we have already learned about if and if…else statements, we haven't really seen these in action. This is where logics are made, and we are going to use this example to develop a good understanding.

The Logic Statements

Whenever logic statements are mentioned, we programmers immediately think about the if and else conditional statements. You see, for a logical decision to take place, a condition must be met. If that condition is not met, another logical decision is then carried out.

Let me explain this in a very simple manner. If it is hot outside, we will then wear summer clothes. If it is snowing outside, we will then wear winter clothing. Depending on which condition is true, we will take the appropriate action as a result. With me so far? Good! Time to move on.

Now, the code shows the if and else in action. Notice how these conditional statements are written using a set of curly braces. This is because every conditional statement or loop statement will have their own unique block of code.

For this situation, we have the following:

```
if (buttonState == HIGH) {
digitalWrite(ledPin, HIGH);
}
else {
digitalWrite(ledPin, LOW);
}
```

Now, what's going on here? You see, the first condition states that "if" the buttonState is perfectly equal to HIGH, meaning giving a higher voltage or ON, it should then turn the ledPin ON. Therefore, if you upload this sketch and push that button, the program will detect that your buttonState changed from 0 to something else that is higher in nature. This is because with the push of a button, voltage will pass through it, and the reading will be higher than 0. As a result, the program will then pass a high voltage through the ledPin and that will effectively turn the light on.

However, if this condition isn't true, the program will simply skip the entire block of code and move on to the next condition. Here, we only have one more condition, which is the else condition. If the above isn't true, the LED will switch off. As soon as you push that button again, the voltage count through the button will lower itself, and it will be recorded as LOW. The program will notice that and it will switch the LED off as a result.

The While Loop in Action

For this, we will load up yet another sketch.

1. Go to File
2. Hover your mouse over Examples
3. Go to 05.Control
4. Click on WhileStatementConditional

Once again, to help you save time, here is the entire code.

The circuit:

- photoresistor connected from +5V to analog in pin 0
- 10 kilohm resistor connected from ground to analog in pin 0
- LED connected from digital pin 9 to ground through 220 ohm resistor
- pushbutton attached from pin 2 to +5V
- 10 kilohm resistor attached from pin 2 to ground

```cpp
const int sensorPin = A0;
const int ledPin = 9;
const int indicatorLedPin = 13;
const int buttonPin = 2;


// These variables will change:
int sensorMin = 1023;
int sensorMax = 0;
int sensorValue = 0;


void setup() {
 pinMode(indicatorLedPin, OUTPUT);
 pinMode(ledPin, OUTPUT);
 pinMode(buttonPin, INPUT);
}

void loop() {

 while (digitalRead(buttonPin) == HIGH) {
 calibrate();
 }

 digitalWrite(indicatorLedPin, LOW);

 // read the sensor:
 sensorValue = analogRead(sensorPin);

 sensorValue = map(sensorValue, sensorMin, sensorMax, 0, 255);

 sensorValue = constrain(sensorValue, 0, 255);

 analogWrite(ledPin, sensorValue);
}

void calibrate() {

 digitalWrite(indicatorLedPin, HIGH);

 sensorValue = analogRead(sensorPin);


 if (sensorValue > sensorMax) {
 sensorMax = sensorValue;
```

```
    }

    if (sensorValue < sensorMin) {
    sensorMin = sensorValue;
    }
    }
```

Here, we have quite a few things going on. Let's walk through each one of those so that we don't get intimidated or confused.

You see, we start just like we did previously, by defining constants and some integer variables.

We have a sensor that is connected to A0, and LED that is connected to 9, the built-in LED that is on pin 13, and a push button on pin 2. We want these values to remain constant, hence the following:

```
const int senorPin = A0;
const int ledPin = 9;
const int indicatorLedPin = 13;
const int buttonPin = 2;
```

Next, we have a few variables we need to set up and declare before we move towards the void setup() part. We want the sensor's minimum reading to be 1023, and the max to be 0. Don't worry, that's how you define these. Next, we also want the sensor value itself to be set to 0.

```
int sensorMin = 1023;
int sensorMax = 0;
int sensorValue = 0;
```

With that sorted, it is time to move towards the next part. This is where we will set our LED pins as outputs and we will change the push-button pin to work as an input.

```
void setup() {
pinMode(indicatorLedPin, OUTPUT);
pinMode(ledpin, OUTPUT);
pinMode(buttonPin, INPUT);
}
```

That will set everything for us just as we want that. Now, we start the real program itself. Straight away, we see the while loop in action.

```
while (digitalRead(buttonPin) == HIGH) {
calibrate();
}
```

Remember, when we use while loops, the system will first check to see if the condition defined is true. If it is, it will carry out the instructions that follow in the block of code. Here, we have set a condition that literally says, "For as long as the buttonPin is equal to HIGH, run the calibrate function."

Therefore, as long as we hold the push button pressed, the value will change to HIGH and this condition will remain true. As soon as we let go off the button, the calibration process will terminate as the condition will no longer be true.

The calibrate function is something you have just created yourself. It is defined by a block of code that says the following:

```
void calibrate() {
```

```
// turn on the indicator LED to indicate that calibration is happening:
digitalWrite(indicatorLedPin, HIGH);
// read the sensor:
sensorValue = analogRead(sensorPin);

// record the maximum sensor value
if (sensorValue > sensorMax) {
sensorMax = sensorValue;
}

// record the minimum sensor value
if (sensorValue < sensorMin) {
sensorMin = sensorValue;
}
}
```

Now, let's look at this in detail, shall we? The very first line tells Arduino that you want to create a function that is called calibrate. You don't want any arguments to be passed through it and it returns no information when executed.

Since this is a void statement, and we are technically defining a function, it opens and closes with curly braces, meaning that it will house an entire block of code within it. It can be multiple blocks of code, but we will stick with one for now.

We start with the digitalWrite() function. We want to change the indicatorLedPin from LOW to HIGH. This means that this will turn the indicator LED on whenever calibration is taking place. To be more precise, whenever the calibrate function is called upon and working, this built-in LED will light up.

Next, we want to take a reading from the sensor itself. This is a problem. We can't just store a value because we think that is what the reading is. We need to let the sensor read and find that value for us. To do that, we do the following:

sensorValue = analogRead(sensorPin);

Remember, the = is the assignment operator. What this will do is first check what value lies on the right side of the assignment operator. Here, it will see analogRead(sensorPin), which is to say "Get a reading from the sensorPin that is attached." It will then come back with a reading, and it will be that reading that will then be assigned to the sensorValue. See how it works?

We aren't done yet. We have another set of conditional statements at our hand. Let's take a look.

If (sensorValue > sensorMax) {
sensorMax = sensorValue;
}
If (sensorValue < sensorMin) {
sensorMin = sensorValue;
}

Pretty self-explanatory, no? We want to ensure that our maximum and minimum values keep changing and reflect the updated information correctly. Since our program will set the minimum and maximum values by 1023 and 0 respectively, these will go on to change whenever calibration takes place. We want to ensure we capture these readings and are not stuck with 1023 and 0.

This is where these two conditional statements will help us greatly. If the sensorValue, which was just read by the analogRead() function, is higher than the sensorMax value of 0, which we set at the start, the program will assign this new value to sensorMax. Similarly, if the sensorValue, picked up ealier, is lesser than the sensorMin, which was set to 1023, the new value will then be assigned to sensorMin.

Great work trying to keep up there. It is very easy to get lost in all this technical mumbo jumbo, but I am glad you made it through. Since we have the function and these little readings out of the way, we are left with one part. While this was essentially in the middle of the code, I didn't want to confuse you by introducing something completely new and technical first.

```
void loop() {

while (digitalRead(buttonPin) == HIGH) {
calibrate();
}

digitalWrite(indicatorLedPin, LOW);

// read the sensor:
sensorValue = analogRead(sensorPin);


sensorValue = map(sensorValue, sensorMin, sensorMax, 0, 255);


sensorValue = constrain(sensorValue, 0, 255);


analogWrite(ledPin, sensorValue);
}
```

First, go ahead and open your IDE:
1. Go to Help
2. Click on References

This is a great place where you can familiarize yourself with all that may seem too technical or something that may not be covered in this book. It is a great tool for beginners and professionals a like and offers a very detailed look into whatever it is that you may be searching for.

This newly-opened web page will show you all that Arduino has to offer. You will see familiar names, such as digitalRead() and digitalWrite(), as well as pinMode(), analogRead(), and so on. The one we are looking for now is something called map. You should be able to locate it under Math. It should read map().

Since our code is using this function, it is essential that we familiarize ourselves with what this function does. Go ahead and click on map() to open up another page, According to the description on Arduino.cc, map() "Re-maps a number from one range to another. That is, a value of fromLow would get mapped to toLow, a value of fromHigh to toHigh, values in-between to values in-between, etc."

Okay, that's quite cryptic. Let me try and simplify that for you. The map() function simply maps a number, from a given range to another. This function is able to take up to five parameters (the instructions that go within the parenthesis). These are:

1. A numeric value
2. Current low
3. Current high
4. Target low
5. Target high

When your system has this information, it is then able to scale the value between the given target range, and it uses math to do that.

"It all sounds gibberish to me!"

Let's take a practical approach to this. When you attach a sensor, you have no way of telling what values it will generate or return to you. You will not even know if these values fall in a range in your given data set. Arduino comes to our rescue here. It is able to incrementally increase the output for one of its many pins. The incremental range is one bit in nature, meaning it is between 0 to 255 number range. As long as our sensor is reflecting a value between this range, our chip will go on to respond how we want it to. If it isn't, something is off. This is why we carry out calibration to ensure our sensors and other connected instruments are aligned and properly functioning before we carry out the actual test.

Furthermore, if you read closely, the Arduino's website states that the map function will NOT change values if they fall outside the specified range. Therefore, if a value reading goes beyond our specified range, the map() function is no good. To counter that problem, we use another function called constrain().

Go back to the main reference page and now search for constrain() function and click on it.

This description is a lot easier to understand. This function literally constrains a number to be within a range. This means that if we were experiencing an fluctuation or a spike in numbers, this function will come into action and bring that number down or up to the specified range, allowing the map() to carry on doing its job.

The constrain() function takes in three parameters. It takes a value, a minimum and a maximum number. If the value falls under the specified range, the value will be left alone. However, if it falls below or above the maximum or minimum number, it will be set to the nearest number, which could be the max or the min.

Once again, the Arduino chips usually deal with numbers ranging from 0 to 255 as pin output intensity. If the number goes up, this could affect our board, which is why the constrain() function acts as a safeguard, just to keep the numbers in range and keep our board healthy.

The For Loop

We already know what a loop does. However, it is time to learn how a for loop works. Since we are at a stage where we are discussing some good examples, it is a good time to dive into this one and see what's what.

The for loop is used to count something a number of times through a given sequence. It is also used to initialize the pins on your board.

The for loops come with their own unique variables. These variables are created on the go and have no effect on any other variable apart from the ones called upon explicitly. Through for loops, you can modify variables so that they keep changing the condition every time a loop finishes. This is something important because if the variable remains the same, the loop will continue to work endlessly and we don't want that to overload our system and crash the party, or in this case the program.

for (variable; condition; increment/decrement) {}

This is how you typically write a for loop. The for loop needs three things to work with.

1. It needs a local variable, which is generally the unique for loop variable we will create.
2. It needs a condition that it can check with. If this is true, it will continue running.
3. It needs an increment or decrement, depending on what we are doing with it.

Without any of these, the for loop will not execute properly. General practice would see programmers name this unique variable with single characters or names, to denote what the loop is actually doing here. If you are going to cycle through all of your pins, you can name it thisPin. This is a good name because it makes immediate sense for the programmer. Any other programmer will look at your code and be able to tell what you are doing. However, there is an exception here. If you are going to index through a list of numbers, which we call an array, this name won't be feasible. Don't worry, we will be going through arrays shortly.

For the condition, we call upon our old friends, the comparison operators. Therefore, we use the >, <, ==, >=, <=, != and so on. Then, we have our increments or decrements. We need these because these will change the value after every successful loop iteration. Remember, if there is no change, the program will not go any further.

Fellow C++ programmers, you would be pleased to know that Arduino is based on C++, and this means that you can use the same incremental symbols you would generally use for all your C++ projects. However, for the benefit of those who have never programmed before, here's how you do things.

```
for (int sampleValue; sampleValue >1; sampleValue++) {
digitalWrite(ledPin, HIGH);
}
```

Let's see what's going on here. First, we declared an integer variable and named it sampleValue. Then, we set a condition, which is sampleValue is greater than 1. Finally, we gave it an increment. The two plus signs simply means increase the variable by a value of 1. If all works, the ledPin will be switch to HIGH.

Take a minute and try to see if you can spot a problem here. Found it? Great! You see, the condition says that the sampleValue must be greater than 1 in order for this code to work. There are only one of two possible outcomes here:

1. The code will not execute since sampleValue has no value.
2. The code will continue to run forever because with every increment, the value of sampleValue will always be greater than 1.

See the problem? This is why it is very important that we first visualize the loop in our head, write it down and workout what needs to increase or decrease, what values we will be dealing with, so that we can use the correct terms and set the right condition.

There are a few ways you can make this loop work.

1. change the condition to something like sampleValue <10. This would allow the program to run through nine iterations at most before the condition no longer remains true.
2. Change the value of the sampleValue to 10, and change the increment to decrement by using two minus signs (--). This will start counting it backwards until the condition is no longer true.

There are other variations to the above as well. All you need is to know what needs to be done to make your for loop work without running into errors.

The Arrays

You will find many instances where you will need to store a lot of numbers. While you can always create separate variables for them, it can often be a hassle. Let's say you want to record all the temperature readings from your temperature sensor, you wouldn't record the temperature by declaring a new variable every single time it changes, would you? That would take ages and a lot of space. Instead, to help us out, we have something called arrays.

An array is nothing more than a collection of variables. These are accessed via index numbers. To create an array, we use the following syntax:

int nameOfArray [number of indexes you want to store];

So, a more practical way to do this would look like this:

int tempReadings [5];

What this does is declare tempReading as an array that holds integer values, five of them. If you already know the numbers you would want to store in an array, you can do something like this:

int tempReading [] = {87, 91, 84, 99, 101};

This will store all these five integer values into the tempReading array. These are stored using index numbers.

The index numbers work a little different than your regular numbers. If I was to ask you to tell me the index number of the value 87, you would probably say, "That's index number 1," but you would be wrong. You see, the index number starts from 0 instead of 1. Therefore, if you were to break the numbers above down into their relative index numbers, it would be like this:

Index number 0 = 87
Index number 1 = 91
Index number 2 = 84
Index number 3 = 99
Index number 4 = 101

Here's a rule of thumb for you to remember:

Index number = position of value – 1

Therefore, if you were to look for the third number, it's index value would be 3 – 1, which is two. With that sorted, let's come back to the arrays.

Arrays are defined using the square brackets [], whereas the numbers that are stored within an array are defined under curly braces {}. You separate every number with a comma and a space. That means, the next time you see something with [] in front of it, that's an array.

To call upon these individual values, you can use the indexing method. Say, I want to access the value that lies on index number 3. To do that, I will type:

tempReading[3];

Now, Arduino will run through the array and find whatever value is parked on index number three and use it. Of course, this isn't a good example to showcase that, so let's change things a bit.

Let's say we want to store the pin numbers 2,5,7,9, and 11 in an array called myLedPins. To do that, we will type the following:

int myLedPins[5] = {2, 5, 7, 9, 11};

This will create an integer array named myLedPins and store the values within it. Now, let's say we want to create a variable and give it a value of pin number 7. This variable is called 'x,' for demonstration purposes. To do this, we will do the following:

x = myLedPins[2];

This will go on to fetch the value from index number two of the myLedPins array, which happens to be pin number seven. As a result, pin number seven will be assigned to variable x.

Here's a quick question, what would the following code do?

digitalWrite(myLedPins[3], HIGH);

Did you guess it yet? That's correct! It will change pin number 9 to HIGH. You see? Array is a really useful datatype that you will be using quite a lot in your future projects. "What if I don't know how many variables an array must hold?"

Well, there is a way to sort that out as well. Have a look at the following code:

int myLedPins[];

What this did was to create and initialize the array right away. While we did not specify how many index numbers or values it must hold, we were able to create this successfully. Now, every time you want to add a value to this array, you can do so easily. How?

myLedPins[0] = 3;
myLedPins[1] = 4;

And you can carry on for as long as you like. Time now for us to see arrays in a more practical way by using one of the pre-made sketches.

1. Go to File
2. Hover on Examples
3. Choose 05.Control
4. Click on Arrays

The code this will load up looks like this (without the comments).

```
int timer = 100;
int ledPins[] = {
 2, 7, 4, 6, 5, 3
};
int pinCount = 6;
void setup() {
for (int thisPin = 0; thisPin < pinCount; thisPin++) {
      pinMode(ledPins[thisPin], OUTPUT);
 }
}
void loop() {
for (int thisPin = 0; thisPin < pinCount; thisPin++) {
      digitalWrite(ledPins[thisPin], HIGH);
 delay(timer);
      digitalWrite(ledPins[thisPin], LOW);
```

```
}
```

```
for (int thisPin = pinCount - 1; thisPin >= 0; thisPin--) {
        digitalWrite(ledPins[thisPin], HIGH);
 delay(timer);
 digitalWrite(ledPins[thisPin], LOW);
 }
}
```

Okay. We begin by declaring a timer variable and assigning it a value of 100. Here, it is important to note that the higher this number is, the slower the timing is. Next, we declare another variable ledPins, but this is an array, which is why the empty square brackets. We assigned it the values of 2, 7, 4, 6, 5, and 3. These are pins that are attached to the LEDs.

Finally, we declare another variable pinCount and set it to 6, which is the total number of pins, or the length of the array.

In the void setup() part, we are using a for loop to initialize each pic as an output instead of us doing it manually for each one of them.

```
for (int thisPin = 0; thisPin < pinCount; thisPin++) {
pinMode(ledPins[thisPin], OUTPUT);
}
```

Here, the for loop has a unique variable thisPin. The loop will run for as long as thisPin holds a value lesser than the pinCount value, which is 6. Remember, I mentioned that pinCount is essentially the length of our array, and arrays use index numbers. Therefore, the maximum iterations for this would be six.

First, it will start with thisPin value as 0. The pinMode function will then iterate through the ledPins array, with the index number as 0 as well, since thisPin holds 0 value in the first iteration. The zero index means first value, which is pin 2. Therefore, pin 2 will be initialized as an OUTPUT pin. It will continue doing this all the way through to index number 5, which happens to be the last pin number of our array. After this, the for loop will stop because the condition defined will no longer be true. Six is not lesser than six, hence the condition will now be false and the loop will break.

In one swift move, you were able to initialize all the pins.

Well, that's all good, but how do you work with sensors? I mean, there are like a million of them already, each having something unique to offer. That is exactly where we are headed next.

Chapter 10: Sensors – How to Work Them

Arduino offers a range of sensors to choose from, each one offering something new, something unique. They all come with their own unique functions and can often be used together to create something more complex in nature.

Arduino creators designed the entire language to work seamlessly with sensors. The best thing is that these sensors don't cost you a fortune either. Recall how the entire philosophy behind the creation of Arduino was affordability.

To give you a taste of some of the sensors you can easily grab, here are some:

- IR infrared obstacle avoidance sensor module
- Microphone sensor
- Ultrasonic module
- Soil hygrometer detection module
- Soil moisture sensor
- Photoresistor sensor module
- Digital barometric pressure sensor board
- Motion sensor module

- Digital thermal sensor module
- Temperature sensor module
- Light detection module
- MQ-2gas sensor module
- Wi-Fi module
- Accelerator module
- Speed sensor module

I can go on and on, but the list would get really long. Of course, some of these sensors are really easy to operate than others, which is why it is best to do your homework first before you order your first sensors, apart from the ones that you already get in your starter kit.

For sensors, it is important to understand how to read analog signals. This is something you would want to learn in order to fully understand and make use of sensors.

If you have never seen an analog signal before, it is a wave-like signal that we can easily see using the Arduino IDE's Serial Plotter. There, you can see these waves fluctuating and in action. If you dial up the input or output, they go higher. If you lower these, they go lower. What the serial plotter does is plot the pattern of analog signals to give users visual feedback of the signal itself.

Analog inputs are generally the results of change in some factor. Your sensors pick up different readings and they keep changing, hence the waves that are formed. Similarly, if you use a photoresistor, you can use the serial plotter to see the difference in light intensity that the photoresistor picks up.

If you have a multimeter, you can use it to measure the voltage on your sensors. In fact, you can pretty much measure all other external factors as long as you use the appropriate sensor. Therefore, things like temperature, light, power, humidity, speed, and many others can easily be mapped out and displayed on the plotter.

Your Arduino UNO R3 comes with six pins for analog purposes, meaning that these are designed specifically to carry analog signals back and forth and to help you map these out. These are located on pins A0 to A5. Using these pins, you can measure voltages that are very accurate in nature.

Knowing How to Use Sensors

Now that you know how the theory works, let's get into using the sensors and really get practical here.

For this example, we will be using a temperature sensor. You should have already received one in your starter kit. If not, you can order one and try this exercise out yourself. We will be creating a very simple device that is meant to measure the temperature. For this, we will not be using the Arduino IDE.

A temperature sensor is sensitive, but what's more sensitive is the transistor that it comes with. That is made using silicon, which is extremely reactive to temperature changes. Don't worry; It won't burst. We actually want a highly reactive element since we really want even the slightest changes in temperature to be recorded.

Your temperature sensor comes with these:
1. A ground leg (GND) that you can connect with a ground point.
2. An Input (vin) which has an operating voltage between 2.2V to 5.5V.
3. A signal leg (center or vout) which gets the measurement for us.

Now, let's set this up and see what's what. For this one, you will need:

1. A multimeter
2. Two AAA 1.5V batteries
3. A temperature sensor (LM35 or TMP35)

Here are the steps to assemble this little device using your Arduino UNO R3 board.

1. Insert the AAA batteries into the battery holder that came with the kit. This should now give you a total voltage of 3V that you can check using the multimeter.
2. Connect your battery holder's red wire to the sensor's input (vin) leg.
3. Connect your battery holder's black wire to the sensor's ground (GND) leg.
4. Turn your multimeter on and dial it into voltage mode
5. Next, connect your multimeter's black probe with the ground (GND) leg
6. Connect your multimeter's red probe with the vin leg
7. Take a note of the reading on the multimeter. You should be getting 0.76 volts.
8. Next, place your hand on the sensor and observe the change in voltage.

Why do you think that is happening? You see, our skin and blood are warm in nature. The closer we get to the sensor, the more warmth it detects, hence the increasing number of voltage.

Here's another example to look into, and this one involves the use of Arduino's IDE. For this experiment, we will be controlling the intensity of light using the potentiometer you received in your starter kit. For this, we will need:

1. Your Arduino UNO R3 board
2. A breadboard
3. One LED
4. One 560 Ohm resistor
5. Wires
6. One 10 KOhms potentiometer

Let's get started and connect these things together using the step-by-step guide as follows:

1. On your breadboard, connect the small leg of your LED to D25 and the longer one to D26
2. Connect your 560 ohm resistor to C26 and C30
3. Next, connect your 10 KOhms potentiometer to C34, C35, and C36
4. Connect one end of a black wire to b25 and – terminal on row 24
5. Connect a black jumper lead in the negative terminal on row 25, and ground using GND
6. Use a blue jumper lead and connect that to A30, ~9
7. Use a red jumper lead and connect to A35, 5V
8. Use a yellow jumper lead and connect on A35, A0
9. Finally, a black jumper lead to A36, - terminal on row 37

With that sorted, we move towards the coding.

Go ahead and create a new file. This should load up a blank template for you to work with. Now, use the following code:

```
const int sensPin = A0;
const int LedPin = 9;
int inutValue = 0;
int outputValue = 0;
void setup() {
Serial.begin(9600);
}
```

```
void loop() {
inputValue = analogRead(analogPin); //This will read value from your potentiometer
Serial.print("Input: "); // this will print "Input"
Serial.println(inputValue); //pring inputValue
outputValue = map(inputValue, 0, 1023, 0, 255)
Serial.print("Output: ");
Serial.println(outputValue);
analogWrite(ledPin, outputValue);
delay(1000);
}
```

The analogRead() function that we have used here will read the voltage as an analog signal, not a digital signal. It will also convert the values to digital values ranging from 0 to 1024. We call such a conversion as ADC, or analog to digital conversion.

Now go ahead and upload this sketch to your Arduino board. Before using your potentiometer, be sure to turn on to Serial Plotter on your IDE to see these waves in action. Use the potentiometer and see how the waves change.

Diving Deeper

Let's now create something a little more complex than just a potentiometer that changes the voltage and creates some waves on the plotter.

We will need:
1. Arduino board – Your UNO R3 is perfect
2. Breadboard – half size
3. Five jumper wires
4. Temperature sensor
5. USB A to B cable

Let's first create the circuit.
1. Use a black wire to connect to GND and negative terminal on row 30 (This should be in blue and on the far-right side of the breadboard)
2. Connect one red wire to 5V and the other end to a positive terminal on row 30 (shown as red on the far right)
3. Connect your temperature sensor to F5, F6, and F7
4. Connect a yellow jumper wire to J5 and A0
5. Connect a red wire to J7 and a positive terminal on 9

Next, connect your board to your computer using the USB cable. Create a new project on your IDE.

Type in the following code:

```
const int tempPin = A0;
void setup() {
Serial.begin(9600);
}
void loop() {
float, degreesC, voltage, degreesF; // declaring multiple variables
voltage = getVoltage(tempPin);
degreesC = (voltage – 0.5) * 100.0;
degreesF = degreesC * (9.0/5.0) + 32.0;

Serial.print("Voltage is:");
```

```
Serial.print(voltage);
Serial.print("Deg C is:");
Serial.print(degreesC);
Serial.print("Deg F is:");
Serial.print(degreesF);

delay(1000);
}
float getVolrate(int pin) {
return (analogRead(pin) *0.004882814);
}
```

Go ahead and upload the sketch to your Arduino UNO R3 and open up your serial plotter. Now, you will be gauging the temperature as well as the fluctuations as they happen.

It does make you feel excited seeing all of that taking shape and producing some results, right? Well, don't worry because I have 10 extremely juicy and creative projects for you to work with. Besides, they will provide you with a good opportunity to master Arduino. For now, I encourage you to browse through all the available sketches and try and tinker with those to gain some confidence. I know, connecting these wires and the sensors might have made you feel a bit scared. You might have thought, "What if I connect it wrong?" The best way to learn is to experience. Yes, you may not connect a wire or two right, and you can expect a sensor or two to go bust, but that's just part of the journey. The people behind Arduino knew that would happen, which is why they wanted affordability to be their number one priority. With that said, Move on to the next section of the book where I bid you farewell, and leave you with 10 extremely creative ideas to work on.

You are more than welcome to browse through YouTube to find tutorials on these projects, or choose something a bit more interesting. Whatever the case, do not stop practicing.

Conclusion

Arduino is meant to be creative, fun, and something everyone can pick and learn. It is simple, and nimble, but it can often create some of the most fascinating designs and projects the world has ever seen. You would be surprised at just how much you can go on to achieve with the use of simple breadboards and Arduino boards.

Many developers and designers rely on Arduino to first carry out the essential steps, understand the circuitry, and then scale those ideas into something larger than life. That is the power of Arduino.

Arduino may have seemed like an impossible task to achieve, an impossible language to learn, but with a bit of patience and practice, you were able to learn the basics. Of course, there is a lot more that is to be learned. You would have seen that we haven't covered quite a few of the functions and features, but that is because they are far too advanced for beginners. I didn't want to burden you with more than what you have already learned. What remains now is for you to practice and explore your hobby or passion for this incredibly vast and almost limitless field.

Before I go further, here are the 10 projects I promised you. Try these out on your own, browse through YouTube and learn how they are done, or just check the community pages to find out more about how others have done it.

1. The Buzz Wire game – This is my absolute favorite. It is a great game, a great project, and it is extremely rewarding. If you haven't seen a buzz wire game before, the object is to pick up a piece of cable with exposed wires at one end that form a loop, and take it to the finishing point without touching the wire the loop covers. It is a lot trickier than it sounds, but it is an extremely cool and fun project to get started with. It is simple to design, but extremely fun to have around.
2. Creating your own Arduino game controller – Yes! You can do that. If you are a gamer, you would be thrilled to know that game controllers owe their success to Arduino boards. Many developers and designers have used Arduino at some point in their careers to bring out the best of the controllers the world has to offer. However, for this project, you will also need to download Unity 3D, which is a famous game engine. It is available to download for free, so you don't have to worry about breaking your bank there. However, to operate Unity 3D, you will need to learn C# programming language, that is if you are trying to create complex games. If you are only looking to create simpler games, you don't need to learn the language at all. You can connect your own Arduino controller with Unity 3D and play the game when you like.
3. The Arduino MIDI controller – Musicians, rejoice! We have something for us here as well. You can actually use Arduino to create your own custom-built MIDI controller. Whether you like to just fool around with MIDI controllers or actually create music, you can do that using nothing but a few simple items and your Arduino UNO R3. Of course, don't expect to create a full 88-keys MIDI controller, not yet at least.
4. Smart Locks – Ever heard of RFID smart keys? These are the ones that are blank, but when you scan these cards with an RFID Card reader, the gates unlock or the safe opens. You can actually create your own RFID system using Arduino and secure your goods, and many other items easily.

5. Traffic Lights – This is quite a simple one, but it may interest the younger members of the society. All you need are three LEDs, some resistors, wires, and a breadboard.
6. The Arduino Alarm – Arduino allows you to create simple alarm systems. These are triggered using the ping sensors. Install these around your residence and you have yourself a working home security system, saving you a lot of money.
7. Mood Lamp – Who doesn't like a mood lamp? Well, now you can create your own.
8. Prank Remote – Arduino is meant to be fun, and what's more fun than pranking your best friend or your beloved one? Be sure to check this one out.
9. The Classic Pong Game – Remember the old classic game where we used lines to defend our posts and hit the ball back? Well, you can recreate that classic game using Arduino and its IDE.
10. The LED cube – This has millions of iterations. You can create your own LED cube, and with relative ease. Just pop on to Google and search for LED Cube Arduino to gain some inspiration.

Well, that's about it for now. It is time for me to say goodbye, and hope that this book served its purpose. The world is literally your oyster, and you are only limited by your imagination. The more you browse through the internet, the more ideas you will end up with. Not all ideas are worth pursuing, but hey! If it's interesting enough, never say never.

Arduino is meant to bring out that child within you, and it is just how Arduino is meant to be used. It is just one of the many languages to learn, but it is definitely one that appeals the most because you get something physical to play with and create with. Coding alone can often be very dry and boring, but throw in a few sensors, some servo motors, and you end up working on a robot or a all-wheel-drive miniature vehicle. You can use Arduino in so many different ways, and all of them are worth chasing. However, be sure to know what you can do and what you can't do. Some projects may be very appealing, but they may require you to buy a lot of things.

I always encourage everyone to browse through projects and study them first. If they are affordable and worth investing your money on, then go for it. I hope you have a wonderful time creating all of these projects and many more to come. Until the next time, take care and have fun the Arduino way!

References

Arduino.cc. (n.d.-a). *Arduino Reference*. Arduino.cc.
https://www.arduino.cc/reference/en/language/functions/math/map/

Arduino.cc. (n.d.-b). *Boards*. Arduino Online Shop. https://store-usa.arduino.cc/collections/boards

Arduino.cc. (n.d.-c). *constrain() - Arduino Reference*. **Www.arduino.cc.
https://www.arduino.cc/reference/en/language/functions/math/constrain/**

www.ingramcontent.com/pod-product-compliance
Lightning Source LLC
Chambersburg PA
CBHW060202060326
40690CB00018B/4212